Scottish Histories

KING ROBERT THE BRUCE

Scottish Histories

KING ROBERT THE BRUCE

WAVERLEY
BOOKS

This edition published 2008 by Geddes & Grosset,
David Dale House, New Lanark ML11 9DJ, Scotland

© 2000 Geddes & Grosset

Adapted from a text by A. F. Murison

ISBN 978 1 902407 65 4

Printed and bound in India

Contents

CHAPTER I

THE ANCESTRY OF BRUCE

When Sir William Wallace, the sole apparent hope of Scottish independence, died at the foot of the gallows in Smithfield and was torn limb from limb, it seemed that at last 'the accursed nation' would quietly submit to the English yoke. The spectacle of the bleaching bones of the heroic patriot would, it was anticipated, overawe those of his countrymen who might still cherish perverse aspirations for national freedom. It was a mistaken anticipation. In fifteen years of arduous diplomacy and warfare, with an astounding expenditure of blood and treasure, Edward I had crushed the leaders and crippled the resources of Scotland, but he had inadequately estimated the spirit of the nation. Only six months, and Scotland was again in arms. It is the irony of fate that the very man destined to bring Edward's calculations to nothing had been his most zealous officer in his previous campaign and had, in all probability, been present at the trial – it may be even at the execution – of Wallace, silently consenting to his death. That man of destiny was Sir Robert de Brus, Lord of Annandale and Earl of Carrick.

The Bruces came to Britain with William the Conqueror. The theory of a Norse origin in a follower of Rollo the Ganger, who established himself in the diocese of Coutances in Manche, Normandy, although not improbable is only vaguely supported. The name is territorial, and opinion is more inclined to connect it with Brix between Cherbourg and Valognes.

The first Robert de Brus, or Bruis, on record was probably the leader of the Brus contingent in the army of the William the Conqueror. His services must have been notable, for he died (about 1094) in possession of some 40,000 acres, comprising forty-three manors in the East and West Ridings of Yorkshire and fifty-one in the North Riding and in Durham. The chief manor was Skelton in Cleveland.

The next Robert de Brus, son of the first, received a grant of Annandale from David I whose companion he had been at the English court. This fief he renounced, probably in favour of his second son, just before the Battle of the Standard (1138) on the failure of his attempted mediation between David and the English barons. He died in 1141, leaving two sons, Adam and Robert.

This Robert may be regarded as the true founder of the Scottish branch. He is said to have remained with David in the Battle of the Standard, and whether for this adherence or on some subsequent occasion, he was established in possession of the Annandale fief which was confirmed to him by a charter of William the Lion (1166). He is said to have received from his father the manor of Hert and the lands of Hertness in Durham, 'to supply him with wheat, which did not grow in Annandale'. He died after 1189.

The second Robert de Brus of Annandale, son of the preceding lord, married (1183) Isabel, daughter of William the Lion, obtaining as her dowry the manor of Haltwhistle in Tyndale. His widow married Robert de Ros in 1191. The uncertainty as to the dates of his father's death and his own has suggested a doubt whether he succeeded to the lordship.

William de Brus, a brother, the next lord, died in 1215.

The third Robert de Brus of Annandale, son of William, founded the claim of his descendants to the crown by his marriage with Isabel, second daughter of David, Earl of Huntingdon, younger brother of William the Lion. He died in 1245.

The fourth Robert de Brus of Annandale, eldest son of the preceding lord, was born in 1210. In 1244 he married Isabel, daughter of Gilbert de Clare, Earl of Gloucester. The next year he succeeded to Annandale, and, on his mother's death in 1251, he obtained ten knights' fees in England, her share of the earldom of Huntingdon. He took an active part in public affairs. In 1249–50 he sat as a Justice of the King's Bench, and in 1268 he became Chief Justice of England, but Edward, on his accession (1272), did not reappoint him. He served as Sheriff of Cumberland and governor of Carlisle Castle in 1254–55, and in 1264 he fought for Henry at Lewes and was taken prisoner.

At the same time, de Brus was a prominent figure in the baronage of Scotland. The alleged arrangement of 1238 whereby Alexander II, with the consent of the Scots parliament, appointed de Brus his successor in the event of his dying childless, was frustrated by the king's second marriage (1239) and the birth of a son, Alexander III (1241). As one of the fifteen regents (1255) during the minority of Alexander III, he headed the party that favoured an English alliance, cemented by the young king's marriage with Margaret, daughter of Henry III. At the Scone convention on 5 February 1284 he was one of the Scots lords who recognized the right of Margaret of Norway. The sudden death of Alexander III, however, in March 1286 and the helplessness of the infant queen put him on the alert for the chances of his own elevation.

On 20 September 1286, de Brus met a number of his friends at Turnberry Castle, the residence of his son, the Earl of Carrick. There fourteen Scots nobles, including de Brus and the Earl of Carrick, joined in a bond obliging them to give faithful adherence to Richard de Burgh, Earl of Ulster, and Lord Thomas de Clare (de Brus's brother-in-law), 'in their affairs'. One of the clauses saved the fealty of the parties to the king of England and to 'him that shall obtain the kingdom of Scotland through blood relationship with King Alexander of blessed memory, according to the ancient customs in the kingdom of Scotland approved and observed.' The disguise was very thin. The instrument meant simply that the parties were to act together in support of de Brus's pretensions to the crown when opportunity should serve. It 'united the chief influence of the West and South of Scotland against the party of John de Balliol, Lord of Galloway, and the Comyns.'

There need be no difficulty in connecting this transaction with the outbreak of 1287–88 which devastated Dumfriesshire and Wigtonshire. The party of de Brus took the castles of Dumfries, Buittle and Wigton, killing and driving out of the country many of the lieges. Nothing remains to show by what means peace was restored, but it may be surmised that Edward interfered to restrain his ambitious vassal.

For, by this time, Edward was full of his project for the marriage of the young queen with his eldest son, Prince Edward. The Salisbury convention, at which de Brus was one of the Scottish commissioners, and the Brigham conference, at which the project was openly declared, seemed to strike a fatal blow at the aspirations of de Brus. But the death of the queen, reported early in October 1290, again opened up a vista of hope.

10

When the news arrived, the Scots estates were in session. 'Sir Robert de Brus, who before did not intend to come to the meeting,' wrote the Bishop of St Andrews to Edward on 7 October, 'came with great power, to confer with some who were there; but what he intends to do, or how to act, as yet we know not. But the Earls of Mar and Athol are collecting their forces, and some other nobles of the land are drawing to their party.' The bishop went on to report a 'fear of a general war', to recommend Edward to deal wisely with Sir John de Balliol and to suggest that he should 'approach the March for the consolation of the Scots people and the saving of bloodshed.' The alertness of de Brus and his friends is conspicuously manifest and the foremost of the party of Balliol is privately stretching out his hands for the cautious intervention of the English king.

The Earl of Fife had been assassinated, the Earl of Buchan was dead, and the remaining four guardians divided their influence, the Bishop of St Andrews and Sir John Comyn siding with Balliol, and the Bishop of Glasgow and the Steward of Scotland with de Brus. Fordun describes the balance of parties in the early part of 1291:

'The nobles of the kingdom, with its guardians, often-times discussed among themselves the question who should be made their king; but they did not make bold to utter what they felt about the right of succession, partly because it was a hard and knotty matter, partly because different people felt differently about such rights and wavered a good deal, partly because they justly feared the power of the parties, which was great, and partly because they had no superior that could, by his unbending power, carry their award into execution or make the parties abide by their decision.'

The most prominent competitors were liegemen of Edward, and whether they appealed to warlike or to peaceful methods, the decision must inevitably rest with him.

At the Norham meeting of June 1291, de Brus, as well as the other competitors, fully acknowledged the paramount title of Edward. He had no alternative; he had as large interests in England as in Scotland and armed opposition was out of the question. Availing himself of his legal experience, he fought the case determinedly and astutely. If Fordun correctly reports the reformation of the law of succession by Malcolm, de Brus was, in literal technicality, 'the next descendant'; as son of David of Huntingdon's second daughter, he was nearer by one degree than Balliol, grandson of David's eldest daughter.

But the modern reckoning prevailed. De Brus's plea that he had been recognized both by Alexander II and by Alexander III was not supported by documentary evidence and his appeal to the recollection of living witnesses does not seem to have been entertained. His third position, that the crown estates were divisible, was but a forlorn hope. He must have seen long before November 1292 that an adverse decision was a foregone conclusion. He entered a futile protest. Already, in June, he had concluded a secret agreement with the Count of Holland, a competitor never in the running but a great feudal figure, for mutual aid and counsel; he had also an agreement with the Earl of Sutherland, and probably enough with others. But an active dissent was beyond the powers of a man of eighty-two. Accordingly, he resigned his claims in favour of his son, the Earl of Carrick, and retired to Lochmaben where he died on 31 March 1295 at the age of eighty-five.

The fifth Robert de Brus of Annandale, the eldest son of

the Competitor, was born in 1253. On his return from the crusade of 1269 on which he accompanied Prince Edward, afterwards Edward I, he married Marjory (or Margaret), Countess of Carrick, and thus became by the courtesy of Scotland Earl of Carrick. Marjory was the daughter and heiress of Nigel, the Celtic (if Celtic be the right epithet) Earl of Carrick, grandson of Gilbert, son of Fergus, Lord of Galloway, and she was the widow of Adam of Kilconquhar, who had died on the recent crusade. De Brus is said to have met her accidentally when she was out hunting. Fordun gives the romance as follows:

> 'When greetings and kisses had been exchanged, as is the wont of courtiers, she besought him to stay and hunt and walk about; and, seeing that he was rather unwilling to do so, she by force, so to speak, with her own hand made him pull up, and brought the knight, though very loth, to her castle of Turnberry with her. After dallying there with his followers for the space of fifteen days or more, he clandestinely took the Countess to wife, the friends and well wishers of both parties knowing nothing about it, and the king's consent not having been obtained. And so the common belief of all the country was that she had seized – by force, as it were – this youth for her husband. But when the news came to the ears of King Alexander, he took the castle of Turnberry and made all her other lands and possessions be acknowledged as his lands, for the reason that she had wedded with Robert de Brus without consulting his royal majesty. Through the prayers of friends, however, and by a certain sum of money agreed upon, this Robert gained the King's goodwill and the whole domain.'

It may be, of course, that the responsibility was thrown on the lady in order to restrain the hand of the incensed king. But she was half a dozen years older than de Brus, who was still in his teens and was never distinguished for enterprise.

In any case, she acted only with the legitimate frankness of her time and the marriage put a useful dash of lively blood into the veins of the coming king.

In every important political step, de Brus followed with docility his father's lead. He stood aloof from Balliol and in spite of marked snubbing steadily adhered to Edward. From October 1295, he was for two years governor of Carlisle Castle. After the collapse of Balliol at Dunbar, he is said to have plucked up courage to claim fulfilment of a promise of Edward's, alleged to have been made in 1292 immediately after the decision in favour of Balliol, to place his father eventually on the Scottish throne. The testy reply of 'the old dodger' (*ille antiquus doli artifex*), as reported by Fordun, is at any rate characteristic: 'Have I nothing else to do but to win kingdoms to give to you?' The story, although essentially probable, is discredited by the chronicler's assertion that the promise was accompanied by an acknowledgment on the part of Edward that his decision of the great cause was an injustice to de Brus, the Competitor.

But while de Brus took nothing by his loyalty to Edward, he suffered for his disloyalty to Balliol. He had, of course, ignored the summons of Balliol 'to come in arms to resist the King of England', and consequently Balliol's council had declared him a public enemy and deprived him of his lands of Annandale, giving them to Comyn, Earl of Buchan. At the same time, and for a similar reason, his son Robert was deprived of the Earldom of Carrick which de Brus had resigned to him on 11 November 1292. Annandale, indeed, was restored to de Brus in September 1296, but the state of Scotland was too disturbed for his comfort and he retired to his English possessions, where, for the most part at least, he lived quietly until Edward had settled matters at Strathord.

He then set out for Annandale but died on the way, about Easter 1304, and was buried at the Abbey of Holmcultram in Cumberland.

De Brus left a large family of sons and daughters, most of whom will find conspicuous mention in the story of the eldest brother, Robert, Earl of Carrick, the future king of Scotland.

CHAPTER II

*O*PPORTUNIST VACILLATION

Robert Bruce, the sixth Robert de Brus of Annandale and the seventh de Brus of the Annandale line, was the eldest son of the preceding lord and a grandson of the Competitor. He was born on 11 July 1274. The place of his birth is uncertain – Ayrshire suggests Turnberry; Dumfriesshire suggests Lochmaben. Geoffrey le Baker calls him an Englishman (*nacione Anglicus*) and records that he was 'born in Essex', to which another hand adds 'at Writtle', a manor of his father's. Geoffrey, it is true, like several other chroniclers, confuses Bruce with his grandfather, the Competitor, and he may mean the Competitor although he says the king. Hemingburgh makes Bruce speak to his father's vassals before the Irvine episode as a Scotsman, at any rate by descent. In any case Bruce was essentially, by upbringing and associations, an Englishman. It was probably in, or at any rate about, the same year that Wallace was born. At the English invasion of 1296, they would both be vigorous young men of twenty-two or thereabouts. During most of the next decade Wallace fought and negotiated and died in his country's cause, and built himself an everlasting name. How was Bruce occupied during this national crisis?

Considering the large territorial possessions and wide social interlacings of the family in England, their English upbringing, their traditional service to the English king, their subordinate interest in Scottish affairs, the predominance of the rival house of Balliol and the masterful character of Edward, it is not at all surprising that Robert Bruce should have preferred the English allegiance when it was necessary for him to choose between England and Scotland. On 3 August 1293, indeed, he offered homage to Balliol on succeeding to the Earldom of Carrick. But on 25 March 1296, at Wark, three days before Edward crossed the Tweed, he joined with his father and the Earls of March and Angus in a formal acknowledgment of the English king, and on 28 August he, as well as his father, followed the multitude of the principal Scots in doing homage to the conqueror at Berwick.

With this political subjection one is reluctant to associate a more sordid kind of obligation. Some six weeks later (15 October) it is recorded that 'the King, for the great esteem he has for the good service of Robert de Brus, Earl of Carrick, commands the barons to atterm [adjourn payment of] his debts at the Exchequer in the easiest manner for him.' But the elder Bruce continued to be designated Earl of Carrick in English documents after he had resigned the earldom to his son, and it can hardly be doubted that the debts were his. It is a small matter, indeed, yet one would like to start Bruce without the burden.

Early in 1297, Scotland was heaving with unrest. Edward, while busily arranging 'to cross seas' to Flanders, was also pushing forward preparations for a 'Scottish War'. In May, Wallace and Douglas had summarily interrupted the severities of Ormsby, the English Justiciar, at Scone, and driven him home in headlong flight. About the same time, or somewhat later, Andrew de Moray took the field in Moray, Macduff rose in Fife and Sir Alexander of Argyll set

17

upon the adherents of Edward in the West. On 24 May, Edward had addressed, from Portsmouth, a circular order to his chief liegemen north and south of Forth, requiring them to attend certain of his great officers to hear 'certain matters which he has much at heart', and to act as directed. Bruce was ordered to attend Sir Hugh de Cressingham and Sir Osbert de Spaldington at Berwick. But before the order could have reached him, he must have heard of the expulsion of Ormsby and had probably conceived dynastic hopes from the aspect of affairs. Indeed, he appears to have fallen under English suspicions. For no sooner did the news from Scone reach Carlisle than the bishop and his advisers – the bishop was acting governor in the absence of the elder Bruce at Portsmouth – 'fearing for the faithlessness and inconstancy of Sir Robert de Bruys the younger, Earl of Carrick, sent messengers to summon him to come on a day fixed to treat with them about the King's affairs, if so be that he still remained faithful to the King.'

Bruce duly appeared with a strong following of 'the people of Galloway' and repeated the oath of fealty upon the consecrated Host and upon the sword of St Thomas (à Becket). What more could the bishop want or do? But Bruce went a step further. He summoned his people, says Hemingburgh, and, 'in order to feign colour, he proceeded to the lands of Sir William de Douglas and burnt part of them with fire, and carried off his wife and children with him to Annandale.' For all that, he was already in secret conspiracy with the Bishop of Glasgow, the Steward of Scotland and Sir John of Bonkill, the Steward's brother. Douglas, indeed, presently appears as one of the leaders in the rising, but his relations with Bruce would be subject to easy diplomatic adjustment.

When the time for open action arrived, Bruce appealed to his father's men of Annandale. He repudiated his oath at Carlisle as extorted by force and intimidation and professed a compelling sense of patriotism. The Annandale men deferred reply until the morrow and slipped away to their homes overnight. With his Carrick men, however, he joined the bishop and the steward and began to slay and harry the English in the southwest.

Engrossed in the outfitting of his expedition, Edward delegated the suppression of the Scots to Warenne, Earl of Surrey, the Guardian of Scotland, who sent ahead his kinsman, Sir Henry de Percy, with a strong force. Percy advanced through Annandale to Ayr and two or three days later stood face to face with the insurgents near Irvine. There was dissension in the Scots camp. Sir Richard Lundy went over to Percy, 'saying that he would no longer war in company with men in discord and at variance'. Besides, the English force was no doubt much superior. The insurgent leaders at once asked for terms. The provisional agreement was that 'their lives, limbs, lands, tenements, goods and chattels' should be unharmed, that their offences should be condoned and that they should provide hostages. Such was the humiliating fiasco of 7 July 1297 at Irvine.

So far their skins were safe, and now, on the counsel of the bishop, they appealed to Cressingham and Warenne to confirm the agreement and to vouchsafe an active interest on their behalf with Edward. The full flavour of their pusillanimity can only be gathered from the text of their letter to Warenne.

'They were afraid the English army would attack them to burn and destroy their lands. Thus, they were told for a certainty that the king meant to seize all the middle people of Scotland to send them beyond sea in his war [in Gascony], to their great damage and destruction. They took counsel to assemble their power to defend themselves from so great damages, until they could have treaty and conference with such persons as had power to abate and diminish such kind of injury, and to give security that they should not be exceedingly aggrieved and dishonoured. And, therefore, when the host of England entered the land, they went to meet them and had such a conference that they all came to the peace and the faith of our Lord the King.'

The hostage for Bruce was his infant daughter, Marjory. It would be interesting to know why Douglas failed to provide hostages. It may be that his native obstinacy was aroused by the reprimands of Wallace, who was then in Selkirk Forest and who is said to have displayed intense indignation at the ignominious surrender. Edward ratified the convention, but somehow it was not until 14 November that powers were conferred on the Bishop of Carlisle and Sir Robert de Clifford 'to receive to the King's peace Robert de Brus, Earl of Carrick, and his friends, as seems best to their discretion.'

Midway between the shameful collapse at Irvine and the formal submission at Carlisle lay 11 September 1297 and Wallace's memorable victory at Stirling Bridge. In this great triumph of patriotism Bruce had no part. Neither was he present at the disastrous battle of Falkirk on 22 July 1298. The Scottish chroniclers, indeed, relate the popular story that the English victory was primarily because of Bruce, who, with Bishop Bek, stealthily caught the Scots in the rear and broke up the schiltrons. But this is a complete misconception, possibly the result of a confusion of Bruce with Basset, who, with Bek, delivered the attack on the left wing, not on the rear, or with Bruce's uncle, Sir Bernard, who fought on the English side. In any case, Bruce stands clear of

20

Falkirk. For English chroniclers relate that when Edward withdrew towards Carlisle, Bruce burnt Ayr Castle and fled away into Carrick. Yet it seems all but certain that he was in Edward's allegiance within three weeks before the battle. He had gone over before the result reached him, possibly on learning the dire straits of Edward immediately before or on the strength of a false report of the issue.

The stormy meeting of Scots nobles at Peebles on 19 August 1299 discovers Bruce in a remarkable attitude. One object of the meeting was to choose Guardians of the realm. The discussion was sufficiently heated for Sir John Comyn — the Red Comyn, afterwards slain at Dumfries — to seize the Earl of Carrick by the throat, and his cousin, the Earl of Buchan, to fight with de Lamberton, Wallace's Bishop of St Andrews. The outcome of the wrangle was a purely personal accommodation of an essentially momentary character. It was settled that the Bishop of St Andrews, the Earl of Carrick and Sir John Comyn should be the Guardians, the bishop as principal to have custody of the castles. Bruce, through the Wallace influence, had gained the upper hand. But it must have cost him a pang to consent to act in the name of Balliol.

Bruce, with Sir David de Brechin, returned to the attack of Lochmaben peel where the Scots had been pressing Clifford since the beginning of August. They were unsuccessful in direct assault, but they seriously hindered the victualling of the place by infesting the lines of communication. Bruce would seem to have been in consultation with his colleagues in the Torwood on 13 November when the Guardians, who were then besieging Stirling, dispatched to Edward an offer to cease hostilities on the terms suggested by the King of France. At any rate he is named as Guardian and it is to be

21

noted that the Guardians write 'in the name of King John and the community of the realm'. Edward was compelled to abandon Stirling to its fate and Lochmaben fell at the end of the year. Warenne's December expedition to the western March was a failure. Edward, in fact, had been paralysed by his refractory barons.

During the next two years, while Comyn was doing his best in the field and Wallace was busy in diplomatic negotiation, there is no trace of Bruce in the records. He may have felt it too irksome to pull together with Comyn. But he re-appears – in a new coat – in 1302. On 16 February, Edward, 'at the instance of the Earl of Carrick', granted pardon to a murderous rascal, one Hector Askeloc. And by 28 April 1302, the king had 'of special favour granted to the tenants of his liege Robert de Brus, Earl of Carrick, their lands in England lately taken for their rebellion.' And Bruce attended Edward's parliament towards the end of October.

In the next year or two Bruce manifested special devotion to the English king. When Edward was going north on the campaign of 1303, he ordered Bruce to meet him about the middle of May at Roxburgh with all the men-at-arms he could muster and with 1000 foot from Carrick and Galloway. On 14 July, Bruce received an advance of pay by the precept of Sir Aymer de Valence, the king's lieutenant south of Forth. On 30 December, he is Edward's sheriff of Lanark; on 9 January, he is Edward's constable of Ayr Castle. His star was deservedly in the ascendant by diligent service.

His ardour steadily increased. After the surrender of Comyn and his adherents in February 1304, he threw himself heartily into the pursuit of Wallace. On 3 March, Edward wrote to 'his loyal and faithful Robert de Brus, Earl of

Carrick, Sir John de Segrave, and their company', applauding their diligence, begging them to complete the business they had begun so well and urging them, 'as the cloak is well made, also to make the hood.' Wallace and Sir Simon Fraser were hotly pursued southwards and defeated at Peebles within a week.

About this time Bruce must have received news of the death of his father, probably not unexpected. On 4 April 1304, he was at Hatfield in Essex, from where he wrote to Sir William de Hamilton, the Chancellor, asking him to direct quickly the necessary inquisitions of his father's lands in Essex, Middlesex and Huntingdon as he wished to go to the king with them to do homage. On 14 June, having done homage and fealty, he was declared heir. The succession to the paternal inheritance was happily achieved.

Meantime, on his return north, Bruce had found Edward impatient to launch the siege of Stirling and worked with the energy of gratitude that looks towards favours to come. He undertook the special task of getting up the king's 'engines', siege machines, to Stirling. On 16 April, the king wrote him thanks for sending up some machines and gave particular instructions about 'the great engine of Inverkip', which appears to have been unmanageable for want of 'a waggon fit to carry the frame'. Bruce seems to have been at Inverkip and Glasgow and wherever else any of the thirteen engines were lagging on the road to Stirling. His energy operated in congenial harmony with the king's burning desire for haste.

Yet there was something in the background of all this enthusiastic service. On 11 June, only three days before 'his loyal and faithful Robert de Brus' did homage and fealty to Edward on succession to his father, Bruce met Bishop

Lamberton at Cambuskenneth and formed with him a secret alliance for mutual aid and defence 'against all persons
whatsoever'. Seeing dangers ahead and wishing to fortify
themselves against 'the attempts of their rivals', they engaged
to assist each other to the utmost of their power with counsel and material forces in all their affairs; 'that neither of
them would undertake any important enterprise without
consultation with the other'; and that 'they would warn
each other against any impending danger, and do their best
to avert the same from each other.' No particular motives or
objects, of course, are specified. But the bishop may have
foreseen the likelihood of an invasion of English ecclesiastics, and Bruce would not be slow to perceive the possible
value of the moral support of the Church and of the material aid derivable from the men and lands of the religious
houses of the wide episcopate of St Andrews. At such a moment neither party would affect to forget the Bruce's royal
pretensions. We shall hear of this bond again.

Stirling surrendered on 20 July, the last of the Scottish fortresses that held out against Edward. Wallace, the last centre
of opposition, was a fugitive dogged by emissaries of the
English king. In March the next year, Bruce was with the
king at Westminster, petitioning him for the lands recently
held by Sir Ingram de Umfraville in Carrick – a petition
substantially granted – and he attended Edward's parliament
in Lent. It is hardly any stretch of probability to believe that
he was present in August at the trial and execution of the
illustrious Wallace – the man who, above all others, paved
the way for his elevation to the Scottish throne.

Bruce was now in his thirty-second year. From his
twenty–second year onwards, through the ten years' struggle
of Wallace and Comyn, he was two parts of the time the ac-

tive henchman of Edward and during the other part he is not known to have performed any important service for Scotland. His action during this period – the period of vigorous manhood, of generous impulses and unselfish enthusiasms – contrasts lamentably with the splendour of Wallace's achievement and endeavour and gravely with the bearing of Comyn. One looks for patriotism and heroism; one finds not a spark of either, but only opportunism, deliberate and ignoble, not to say timid – the conduct of a 'spotted and inconstant man'. Yet Bruce was tenaciously constant to the grand object of his ambition. In the light of his kingly career this early period has puzzled historians greatly, but one cannot affect to be surprised that the friendliest critic is compelled to pronounce the simple enumeration of the facts to be 'in truth, a humiliating record'.

CHAPTER III

THE CORONATION OF BRUCE

Stirling surrendered and Wallace a fugitive, Edward went home and meditated measures for the government of the conquered country. While yielding no point of substance, he recognized the policy of conciliation in form. He took counsel with the Bishop of Glasgow, the Earl of Carrick and Sir John de Mowbray and, ostensibly guided by their suggestions, he appointed a meeting of ten Scots and twenty English representatives to be held in London in the middle of July, subsequently postponed to September.

On 23 September, all the representatives were 'sworn on our Lord's body, the holy relics, and holy Evangels, each severally'. The joint commission settled ten points which were embodied in an Ordinance – 'not a logical or methodical document' but 'mixing up the broadest projects of legislation and administration with mere personal interests and arrangements.' First, the official establishment was set forth: Sir John de Bretagne, Junior, Edward's nephew, being appointed King's Lieutenant and Warden, Sir William de Bevercotes Chancellor and Sir John de Sandale Chamberlain. Next, justiciars were appointed, a pair for each of the four divisions of the country. Then a score of sheriffs were named, nearly all Englishmen, although Scots were eligible. Thereafter, the law was taken in hand: 'the custom of the Scots and Brets' was abolished; and the King's Lieutenant, with English and Scots advisers, was 'to amend such of the laws and usages which are plainly against God and reason,' referring difficulties to the king. For the rest, the articles were mainly particular. One of them applied specifically to Bruce: 'The Earl of Carrick to place Kildrummy Castle in the keeping of one for whom he shall answer.' The king confirmed the Ordinance at Sheen. At the same time (26 October), apparently, the King's Council for Scotland – twenty members, including the Bishop of St Andrews, the Earls of Carrick, Buchan and Atholl, Sir John Comyn and Sir Alexander of Argyll – was sworn in. Bretagne was unable to go to Scotland until Lent, and then until Easter. Meantime a commission of four was appointed to act for him, the first commissioner being the Bishop of St Andrews.

The king rejoiced at the sure prospect of peace in Scotland. The country was outwardly quiet. Edward had put on the velvet glove. He had restored submissive barons, knights and lairds to their lands, he had that very day at Sheen doubled the periods within which they might pay their several fines, and he had displayed a general friendly consideration in his Ordinance. A fortnight before (14 October), he had told all the English sheriffs that he wished honourable and courteous treatment to be shown to all Scots passing through their jurisdictions. In a short time, he was contemplating a more complete assimilation of the two countries, to be arranged in a Union convention at Carlisle. But in February next, the whole face of affairs was suddenly transformed by the report that Sir Robert de Brus, Earl of Carrick, had done sacrilegious murder on Sir John Comyn at Dumfries.

The accounts of the train of events leading to the death of Comyn, although agreeing in essentials, vary considerably in details. The Scots story may be told first. Fordun, like his compatriots, colours his narrative deeply with the fanciful glow of Bruce's patriotism. He tells how Bruce 'faithfully laid before Comyn the unworthy thraldom of the country, the cruel and endless torment of the people, and his own kindly project for bringing them relief.' Bruce, he says, 'setting the public advantage before his own,' proposed to Comyn two alternatives: either take you the crown and give me your lands or else take my lands and support my claim to the crown. Comyn chose the latter. The agreement was guaranteed by oaths and embodied in sealed deeds. Eventually, however, Comyn betrayed Bruce's confidence, 'accusing him again and again before the king of England, by envoys and by private letters, and wickedly revealing his secrets.'

Edward acted with restraint: he sounded out Bruce, he even showed him his adversary's letters, he feigned acceptance of his explanations. One evening, however, 'when the wine glittered in the bowl', he expressed his definite determination to put Bruce to death on the morrow. On hearing this, the Earl of Gloucester at once sent Bruce a broad hint in the form of twelve pence and a pair of spurs. Bruce promptly mounted his horse and rode day and night to his castle of Lochmaben. As he was nearing the Border, he met a messenger from Comyn taking to Edward the very bond he had made with Comyn. He struck off the man's head and hurried on his way.

By appointment, he presently met Comyn in the church of the Friars Minorites at Dumfries. He charged Comyn with treachery.

'You lie!' replied Comyn. Whereupon Bruce stabbed him on the spot.

The friars stretched Comyn on the floor behind the altar. 'Is your wound mortal?' he was asked.

'I think not,' he replied. The hopeful answer sealed his fate.' His foes, hearing this, gave him another wound, and thus, on 10 February, was he taken away from the world.'

According to Barbour, the alternative proposal proceeded not from Bruce but from Comyn, which is far from likely, and it was made 'as they came riding from Stirling', presumably – Blind Harry, indeed, expressly says so – when Edward and his barons were going home from the siege. Barbour goes beyond Fordun in stating that Comyn actually rode to Edward and gave him the deed with Bruce's seal. Then, he says, the king 'was angry out of measure and swore that he would take vengeance on Bruce' for his presumption, summoned a council, produced the bond and demanded of Bruce whether the seal was his. Bruce obtained respite until the next day in order to get his seal and compare it with the bond and fled the same night with the it in his pocket.

The embellishments of later writers – the conversion of Gloucester's twelve pence into other coins, the reversal of Bruce's horses' shoes because of the new-fallen snow, and so forth – need not be considered. Barbour makes no mention of an appointment: Bruce rode over to Dumfries where Comyn was staying and the tragedy was enacted. Barbour has the same outline of the interview as Fordun, but he remarks that other accounts were current in his time

A picturesque tradition tells how Bruce, on striking the blow, hurried out of the church to his friends, whereupon Roger de Kirkpatrick and James de Lindsay, seeing his excitement, anxiously inquired how it was with him.

'Ill!' replied Bruce. 'I doubt I have slain the Red Comyn.'

'You doubt!' cried Kirkpatrick. 'I'll mak' siccar' (make sure), and they rushed into the church and buried their daggers in Comyn's body.

29

But if the justiciars were then sitting, and Roger de Kirkpatrick was still one of them, for he and Walter de Burghdon were appointed justiciars for Galloway on 25 October, there may be some difficulty in accepting the tradition.

The English story begins in Scotland and introduces an important element wholly absent from the principal Scottish versions. The English authorities expressly allege a deliberate purpose on Bruce's part to rid himself of his rival. Both Hemingburgh and the Lanercost chronicler state that Bruce sent two of his brothers, with guileful intent, to invite Comyn to an interview – Hemingburgh names Thomas and Nigel.

The fullest account is given by Sir Thomas Gray who wrote in 1355, just half a century later but still twenty or thirty years earlier than Barbour and Fordun. Gray records that Bruce dispatched his brothers, Thomas and Nigel, from Lochmaben to Dalswinton where Comyn was staying to invite him to meet Robert in the church at Dumfries, and, moreover, that he instructed them to fall upon Comyn on the way and kill him – a purpose thwarted by the softening effect of Comyn's kindly reception of the youths.

'Hm!' said Bruce, on hearing their report, 'milksops you are, and no mistake; let me meet him.' So he advanced to Comyn and led him up to the high altar. He then opened the question of the condition of Scotland and invited Comyn's cooperation in an attempt at freedom on the terms already mentioned as contained in the alleged bond between them. 'For now is the time,' he said, 'in the old age of the King.' Comyn firmly refused. 'No?' cried Bruce, 'I had other hopes in you, by promise of your own and of your friends. You discovered me to the King by your letters. Since while you live I cannot fulfil my purpose, you shall have your guerdon!' On the word, he struck Comyn with his dagger, and some of his companions completed the crime with their swords before the altar.

Hemingburgh works up artistically the pacific bearing of Comyn in the face of Bruce's accusations, and this would be likely enough if it is true that Comyn was unarmed and attended by only a small escort. The writer of the Merton manuscript of the *Flores Historiarum*, who says Comyn was unarmed, states that he endeavoured to wrest Bruce's weapon from his hand, that Bruce's men rushed up and freed their leader, that Comyn got away to the altar and that Bruce pursued him and, on his persistent refusal to assent, slew him on the spot.

A distinct English variation occurs in at least five of the records. The Meaux Chronicle states that Bruce, on returning to Scotland after the settlement of the Ordinance, summoned the Scots earls and barons to Scone to consider the affairs of the realm and put forward his hereditary claim. He received unanimous support, except that Comyn stood by his oath of fealty to Edward, rejected Bruce's claim with scorn and at once left the council. The council was adjourned to a future day at Dumfries. Meantime Bruce sent Comyn a friendly invitation. Comyn appeared at Dumfries and was cordially received by Bruce, but still he maintained his objections and again he left the council. Bruce drew his sword and followed him, and ran him through the body in the Church of the Friars Minorites. The Cambridge Trinity College manuscript, it may be noted, states that Bruce sent his two brothers to invite Comyn to meet him at the 'Cordelers' of Dumfries, and Geoffrey le Baker makes Bruce kill Comyn in the midst of the magnates, but these may safely be set aside as grounded on misconceptions.

The English allegation of Bruce's purpose of murder seems to invest with a special interest Blind Harry's casual story with its coincidences and discrepancies. Bruce, says Harry, charged his brother Edward, whom he found at Lochmaben on his arrival, to proceed next day with an armed escort to Dalswinton and to put Comyn to death if they found him. But they did not find him.

When Comyn fell, his followers pressed forward and blows were hotly exchanged. Comyn's uncle, Sir Robert, attacked Bruce himself but failed to pierce his armour (which, the Meaux Chronicler says, he wore under his clothes) and was cut down by Sir Christopher de Seton, probably in the cloister, not in the church. Barbour adds that 'many others of mickle main' were killed in the mêlée, and the statement is amply confirmed.

While this scene was being enacted, the English justiciars were in session in the castle. Bruce and his friends, having overpowered Comyn's adherents, at once went there. The justiciars had prudently barricaded the doors but when Bruce called for fire, instantly surrendered. Bruce spared their lives and allowed them to pass over the Border without harm. According to Hemingburgh, it was only after Bruce had got possession of the castle that he learned that Comyn was still alive after his first wound; whereupon, by order of Bruce, the wounded man was dragged from the vestibule, where the friars were tending him, and slain on the steps of the high altar which was bespattered with his blood.

Comyn was slain (according to the usually accepted date) on 10 February. Less than two months later (5 April) Edward affirmed that he had placed complete confidence (*plenam fiduciam*) in Bruce. The profession may be accepted as sincere, for it is on record under the date of 8 February (the order would have been made some days earlier) that Edward remitted scutage due by Bruce on succession to his father's estates. We may, therefore, put aside the English part of the Fordun and Barbour story and refuse to believe that Edward dallied with Comyn's allegations or was such a simpleton as to let Bruce keep possession of the incriminating bond. But was there a bond at all? It is generally accepted that Edward did hold in his hands a bond of Bruce's, but this bond is usually taken to have been the Lamberton indenture, which is supposed to have come into Edward's possession through the instrumentality of Comyn. Still, there is nothing to show that this indenture was yet in Edward's hands. It may also be gravely doubted whether Comyn would ever have entered into any bond with Bruce. There is much significance in the silence of the English records. Nor is there more than a very slight English indication of any communication about Bruce from Comyn to Edward. It is likely enough, however, that Comyn informed Edward of Bruce's private pushing of his claims, and it may be that the details of the story of a bond were evolved on mere suppositions arising out of the Bruce–Lamberton compact.

The allegation that Bruce deliberately murdered Comyn is the most serious matter. But the English writers do not satisfy one that they had the means of seeing into Bruce's mind, and the allegation may be reasonably regarded as inference, not fact. There can scarcely be any doubt that Bruce resumed the active furtherance of his claims on observation of the declining health of Edward, but without any immediate intention of a rupture. He could hardly have found support enough to counterbalance the far-reaching power of Comyn to say nothing of the power of Edward. Clearly it was of the very first importance that he should, if possible, gain over Comyn. He may have offered Comyn broad lands and high honours. But to expect the practical heir of the Balliol claims to support him was on the face of it all but hopeless, and to speak of patriotism to Comyn would have been nothing less than open insult. Comyn, of course, would stanchly reject Bruce's overtures. Despite all his prudence, Bruce had a hot and imperious temper, and Comyn's obstinacy – it may be Comyn's frank speech – most probably broke down his self-command. If it had been Bruce's deliberate purpose to kill his rival, he would scarcely have chosen a church for the scene or have left the deed to be afterwards completed either by others or by himself. The mere fact that he was totally unprepared for a struggle with Edward tells almost conclusively against the theory of premeditation – unless there was a very clearly compromising bond with Comyn, which is wholly improbable. The bond with Lamberton – the only bond that certainly existed – was capable of easy explanation and was a wholly insufficient reason to urge him to murder a rival whose adherents would make up in bitterness what they lost in leadership.

Nor is there any reason to believe that Lamberton was implicated. True, he was charged, on his own bond, with complicity in the deed. There still exist letters patent dated Scotland's Well, 9 June 1306, in which Lamberton declares to Sir Aymer de Valence, then Edward's lieutenant in Scotland, his anxious desire 'to defend himself in any way the king or Council may devise against the charge of having incurred any kind of guilt in the death of Sir John Comyn or of Sir Robert his uncle, or in relation to the war then begun,' and on 9 August, at Newcastle, he acknowledged the Cambuskenneth indenture. But there is no necessary connection between the compact and the crime, and it is in the last degree improbable that Lamberton had any anticipation whatever of the Dumfries tragedy. His sympathy with Bruce's rising is quite a different consideration.

Having garrisoned Dumfries Castle, Bruce sent out his messengers to raise adherents. The Galwegians having refused to join him, he ravaged their lands and took the castles of Tibbers, Durisdeer and Ayr. But he was not strong enough to keep the castles for more than a very short period. After the first surprise, Comyn's men asserted their superior force and aid arrived from Carlisle. The Lanercost chronicler records that Bruce pursued a Galwegian noble and besieged him in a lake but that the Carlisle contingent raised the siege, compelling Bruce to burn his machines and 'ships' and take to flight. Probably Carlaverock is meant.

Leaving the local struggle to lieutenants, Bruce hastened to Bishop Wishart in Glasgow. At Arickstone, in the upper end of Annandale, Barbour says, he was joined by James of Douglas, who had been staying with the Bishop of St Andrews – a young man destined to play a great part in the history of Bruce. Bishop Wishart joyously received his visitor, cheerfully broke his sixth oath of fealty to Edward, pronounced absolution of Bruce for the murder of Comyn and produced coronation robes and a royal banner. There was nothing half-hearted about the flexible prelate. Already the country was in eager expectation, and Bruce and the bishop proceeded boldly to Scone.

On 27 March 1306, in the Chapel Royal of Scone, the immemorial scene of the inauguration of the kings of the Scots, Robert Bruce was crowned king. The ceremony inevitably lacked certain of the traditional accessories that influenced the popular mind. The venerable Stone of Destiny had been carried off by Edward ten years before. The crown

– if crown there had been – was also gone, and the ancient royal robes – if such there had been – were no longer available. The prescient bishop, however, had provided fresh robes, and a circlet of gold was made to do duty for a crown. Still, there was lacking an important functionary – the person whose office and privilege it was to place the crown on the head of the king. The proper official was the chief of the clan MacDuff. But Duncan, Earl of Fife, was in wardship in England, and again, as on the coronation of Balliol, arose the difficulty of finding a competent substitute. No substitute was forthcoming, and the coronation had to pass with lesser rites.

Two days later, however, this difficulty was dramatically solved. Isabella, Countess of Buchan and sister of the Earl of Fife, had hastened south with an imposing retinue and appeared to claim the honour and privilege of her house. A second coronation – not mentioned by the Scottish writers – was held on 29 March. The wife of a Comyn, closely related to the murdered Sir John, the countess still performed the mystic function. The subsequent punishment of the countess by Edward continued the romance of the occasion, and it may be added here that on 20 March 1307, Edward, at the instance of his queen, pardoned one Geoffrey de Conyers for concealing the coronet of gold with which King Robert was crowned.

The coronation might have been expected to strike the imagination of the Scots and to rally the spirit that cherished the memory of Wallace. Fordun asserts that Bruce's friends in Scotland, as compared with his collective foes, were but 'as a single drop compared with the waves of the sea, or as a single grain of seed compared with the multitudinous sand.' The hyperbole has a considerable basis of fact. Bruce, indeed, was supported at his coronation by the two chief prelates of Scotland, the Bishops of St Andrews and Glasgow, and by the Abbot of Scone;, by strong-handed relatives – his four brothers, Edward, Thomas, Alexander and Nige, his nephew, Thomas Randolph of Strathdon (better known afterwards as Randolph, Earl of Moray) and his brother-in-law, Sir Christopher de Seton (husband of his sister Christian), by the Earls of Lennox, Atholl and Errol, and by such brave men as James de Douglas, Hugh de la Haye (brother of Errol), David Barclay of Cairns, Alexander, brother of Sir Simon Fraser, Walter de Somerville of Carnwath, David de Inchmartin, Robert Boyd and Robert Fleming.

Apart from the episcopal influence, however, the array is not very imposing. Yet how vastly superior to the meagre beginnings of Wallace! Bruce, indeed, lacked one vital source of strength that his great predecessor had – intimate association and sympathy with the common folk. On the other hand, he was admitted, except by the Comyn interest, to be the legitimate sovereign and 'is not the King's name twenty thousand names?' And so it would have been but for his inglorious record. It is only the servile adulation of later writers that has pictured Bruce as animated by patriotism. He was simply a great Anglo-Norman baron in quest of aggrandizement, and it took many years to satisfy the people generally that their interests were safe in his keeping. But he was a man with deep reserves of strength, freed at last from the paralysis of worldly prudence by a sudden shock, and compelled to defend his crown and his life with his back to the wall. Happily, if only incidentally, such self-defence involved the championship of the independence of Scotland.

CHAPTER IV

DEFEAT AND DISASTER: METHVEN AND KILDRUMMY

The new king attacked his task with fiery energy. 'All the English' had not, although many of them had, 'returned to their own land', and Bruce instantly issued a proclamation requiring those who remained to follow those who had gone. According to the Meaux chronicler, he proceeded to expel them, but the particular acts are not recorded. At the same time he imperiously insisted on the submission of such Scots as had not yet joined him. He threw the Perth bailies into prison and required them on pain of death to pay up £54 of the king's Whitsunday rents.

A detailed example of his procedure remains in the memorial of exculpation addressed by Malise, Earl of Strathearn, to Edward. The earl alleges that, on Monday, the day after the coronation, Bruce sent to him the Abbot of Inchaffray, requiring him to repair forthwith to his presence to perform homage and fealty. On his refusal, Bruce, with the Earl of Atholl, entered Strathearn in force, occupied Foulis and dispatched another summons with a safe-conduct to the earl, who took counsel with his followers in the wood of Crieff. Bruce's messenger seems to have been Sir Malcolm de Inverpeffry who had been Edward's sheriff of Clackmannan and Auchterarder and had been one of the first to go over to Bruce. Taking the advice of Sir Malcolm and of his own friends, he went to Bruce, but still he refused to comply with the peremptory demand of submission. Next day, he again met Bruce by appointment at Muthill. In the course of the interview, Atholl, who had been stung by a sharp home thrust of Strathearn's, urged Bruce to break his promise of safe-conduct and give the earl into custody while Atholl's men should go and ravage his lands. Strathearn was taken to Inchmalcolm where he steadily maintained his refusal. Sir Robert de Boyd thereupon advised Bruce to cut off his head and grant away his lands, and to do the same to all others afflicted with such scruples. Strathearn then gave way, and they let him go. The story may be coloured to suit Strathearn's new difficulties, but it may at least be taken as an indication of Bruce's resolute, yet prudent, action.

The memorial further shows that Strathearn was again at issue with Bruce before the Battle of Methven. Bruce sent him a letter, he says, directing him to bring his power to Calder, but instead of obeying the order he communicated the letter to Sir Aymer de Valence, then at Perth, and prepared to follow with his men. Just as he was starting, Bruce came upon him, laid siege to the place where he was and ravaged his lands. At an interview, Strathearn flatly refused to join Bruce in an attack on Valence, and Bruce had to let him go, recalcitrant and unpunished, for the sake of the hostages in the hands of Strathearn's party.

The news of Bruce's revolt and the death of Comyn roused Edward into full martial vigour. He at once dispatched judicious instructions to his officers in Scotland and on the Borders. In March he was directing military supplies to be accumulated at Berwick, and at the beginning of April he commanded the Irish authorities to divert supplies des-

39

tined for Ayr to Skinburness, and to send them 'with the utmost haste', giving 'orders to the seamen to keep the high seas and not to approach the ports of Ayr or Galloway on any account.' On 5 April he issued orders for the immediate muster of the forces of the northern counties at the summons of Valence and Percy.

Having set his army in motion, Edward held a great feast at Westminster at Whitsuntide. By proclamation he invited all youths who had a hereditary claim to knighthood and had the means to campaign to come and receive knighthood along with the Prince of Wales. In the middle of April he had dispatched his clerks to St Botolph's Fair with orders to his sheriffs and other lieges of Southampton and Wiltshire to aid them 'in purchasing 80 cloths of scarlet and other colours, 2000 ells of linen cloth, 400 ells of canvas, 30 pieces of wax and 20 boillones of almonds' for the outfit and entertainment of the new knights. The royal palace could not contain the visitors. The prince and the more noble of the candidates kept vigil in Westminster Abbey, the rest in the Temple. Next day the king knighted the prince and made him Duke of Aquitaine. Then the prince went to Westminster Abbey and conferred knighthood on his companions. The crush before the high altar was so severe that two knights died and many fainted, and the prince ordered in a ring of warhorses to fence off his knights from the crowd. The number of new knights was roughly three hundred.

Then followed a remarkable ceremony. As the king and the knights sat at table a splendid procession entered attended by a train of minstrels in the middle of which were carried two swans in golden nets amid gilt reeds, 'a lovely spectacle to the beholders'. On seeing them, the king chivalrously vowed a vow to God and to the swans – emblems of purity and faith – that he would go to Scotland and, alive or dead, avenge the outrage to Holy Church, the death of Comyn and the broken faith of the Scots. Turning to the prince and the nobles, he charged them by their fealty that, if he should die before accomplishing his vow, they should carry his body with them in the war and not bury it 'till the Lord gave victory and triumph' over the perfidious Bruce and the perjured Scots. One and all, they engaged their faith by the same vow. Trevet adds that Edward further vowed that, when the war in Scotland was successfully ended, he would never more bear arms against Christian men but would direct his steps to the Holy Land and never return from there. 'Never in Britain, since God was born,' says Langtoft, 'was there such nobleness in towns or in cities, except Caerleon in ancient times, when Sir Arthur the King was crowned there.'

The brilliant ceremony over, the prince set out for Carlisle where his army was ordered to be in readiness on 8 July. He was accompanied by a large number of his new-made knights. The king was to follow by slow stages.

Amid the pomp of the gallant ceremonial, Edward's mind was keenly bent on the business of the expedition. Writing to Valence on 24 May, he desires 'that some good exploit be done, if possible, before his arrival.' Two days later (26 May), he is delighted to hear that Valence, then at Berwick, is ready to operate against the enemy and urges him to strike at them as often as possible and in cooperation with the forces at Carlisle. As regards 'the request by some for a safe-conduct for the Bishop of St Andrews', Valence, he orders, 'will neither give, nor allow any of his people to give such.' The bishop, if he pleases, may come to the king's faith and receive his deserts. Let Valence take the utmost pains to secure the bishop's person and also the person of the Bishop of Glasgow and let him send frequent news of his doings.

Valence had a stroke of luck. On 8 June, Edward 'is very much pleased' to learn from him 'that the Bishop of Glasgow is taken, and will soon be sent to him.' The Bishop had been taken in arms on the recapture of Cupar Castle by the English. A week later (16 June), Edward informs Valence that 'he is almost as much pleased as if it had been the Earl of Carrick,' and directs him to send the bishop 'well guarded' to Berwick, 'having no regard to his estate of prelate or clerk.' The order was executed without any undue kindness. The Bishop of St Andrews, however, was still at large. 'I understand from many,' wrote Edward to Valence in the letter of 8 June, 'that the Bishop of St Andrews has done me all the mischief in his power, for, though chief of the Guardians of Scotland appointed by me, he has joined my enemies.'

As yet the edge of Edward's appetite was only whetted. On 12 June, he 'is well pleased to hear that Valence has burned Sir Simon Fraser's lands in Selkirk Forest' and commands him 'to do the same to all enemies on his march, including those who turned against him in this war of the Earl of Carrick, and have since come to his peace as enemies and not yet guaranteed; and to burn, destroy and waste their houses, lands and goods in such wise that Sir Simon and others may have no refuge with them as heretofore.' At the same time, Valence is to spare and honour the loyal, and in particular to compliment the foresters of Selkirk on their loyal and painful service. In successive letters he reiterates the caution to beware of surprise and treason and his anxiety for constant news.

Still more vindictive is his tone on 19 June. He commands Valence to burn, destroy and strip the lands and gardens of

Sir Michael de Wemyss's manors 'as he has found nor good speech nor good service in him,' and this for an example to others. 'Likewise, to do the same, or worse, if possible, to the lands and possessions of Sir Gilbert de la Haye, to whom the King did great courtesy when he was last in London, but now finds he is a traitor': the king will make up the loss to the persons to whom he has granted his lands!

Meantime the pope made his voice heard. On 6 May, he had written to Edward promising to send a nuncio to deal with the Bishop of Glasgow and others, and on 11 May, he had strongly denounced to the Archbishop of York the assumption of the bishop, desiring him to order the culprit peremptorily to come to his Holiness at Bordeaux. The archbishop replied that the bishop had been captured in arms and that the king thought it inexpedient to serve the citation on his prisoner but would send envoys with explanations. On 18 June, the pope addressed a bull to the Archbishop of York and the Bishop of Carlisle directing them to excommunicate Bruce and his adherents and to lay their lands, castles and towns under ecclesiastical interdict until they should purge their offence. Already, on 5 June, according to the London Annalist, the Archdeacons of Middlesex and Colchester had formally excommunicated Bruce and three other knights at St Paul's for the death of Comyn.

However the sacrilegious deed at Dumfries may have affected the attitude of Scotsmen generally to Bruce, it did not produce revulsion in the minds of the more ardent patriots any more than in the minds of Bruce's personal friends. Yet not only the powerful Comyn interest, but also a very large section of the rest of the population, adhered, formally at least, to the English cause. The particular movements of Bruce are not on record, but it appears that his ad-

43

herents were pressing Sir Alexander de Abernethy in Forfar Castle and that Irish as well as Scots allies were active in Fife and Gowrie. The foresters of Selkirk, as we have seen, had stood by Edward and apparently had suffered for their fidelity. Hemingburgh says Bruce 'did great wonders': undoubtedly the impression is that he must have been fighting a strenuous uphill battle. The great mass of the nation, however, was waiting for more definite developments.

In June, Sir Aymer de Valence had advanced from Berwick to Perth. In his company were several prominent Scots – Sir John de Mowbray, Sir Ingram de Umfraville, Sir Alexander de Abernethy, Sir Adam de Gordon, Sir David de Brechin and others who leant to Comyn. He had received to the peace some complaisant Scots whose lands or dwellings lay on his northward route. Bruce probably kept him under observation, retiring before him beyond the Forth and not attempting to bar his progress to Perth.

On 25 June, Bruce, no doubt reinforced, appeared before the walls of Perth and challenged Sir Aymer to come out and fight him or else surrender. Hemingburgh assigns to Valence only 300 men-at-arms and some foot, a smaller force, he says, than Bruce had, but it is most unlikely that Valence was not the stronger, although possibly not by 1500 men, as Barbour alleges. Valence seems to have been ready to accept Bruce's challenge but to have been dissuaded by his Scots friends. Umfraville, says Barbour, advised him to promise battle on the morrow but to attack that night when the Scots were off guard in reliance on his promise. Bruce – 'too credulous', says Hemingburgh – accepted the promise. He was not in a position to establish a siege, and he retired to Methven Wood. His main body set about preparing food and disposed themselves at ease while parties foraged.

In the dusk of the evening, Valence issued from Perth and took Bruce by surprise. It is not to be supposed, as the chroniclers narrate, that Bruce was so inexperienced as to allow his men to lie in careless unreadiness: no doubt many of them would have laid aside their arms, but the very fact that his knights at least fought with loose linen tunics over their armour to hide their distinctive arms would seem to show that they at any rate were prepared. Still they did not expect attack. They promptly rallied, however, and met with vigour the sudden and furious onset. Bruce, keenly realizing the importance of the issue, bore himself with splendid valour. Before his fierce charge, the enemy gave way and, Langtoft says, he killed Valence's charger. Thrice he was unhorsed himself and thrice remounted by Sir Simon Fraser. According to Sir Thomas Gray, he was taken prisoner by John de Haliburton, who let him go the moment he recognized him. Barbour tells how he was hard beset by Sir Philip de Mowbray and was rescued by Sir Christopher de Seton. But the day was going against him and in vain he made a supreme effort to rally his men. He was compelled to retreat. Barbour asserts that the English were too weary to pursue and retired within the walls of Perth with their prisoners, keeping there in fear of the approach of Bruce. But it seems far more likely, as Langtoft relates, that they kept up the pursuit 'for many hours'. The statement of Hemingburgh and others that the English pursued Bruce to Kintyre and besieged and took a castle there, mistakenly supposing him to be in it, is evidently a misconception and a confusion of Dunaverty with Kildrummy.

Bruce lost comparatively few men in the battle – the 7000 of the Meaux chronicle need not be considered – but a number of his ablest supporters were taken prisoners, notably Thomas Randolph, his nephew, Sir Alexander Fraser, Sir David Barclay, Sir Hugh de la Haye, Sir David de Inchmartin and Sir John de Somerville. The Bishop of St Andrews had surrendered to Valence before the battle but had taken care to send his household to fight for Bruce. His calculation is said to have been 'that if the Scots beat the English they would rescue him as a man taken by force for lack of protection, whereas, if the English won the day, they would mercifully regard him as having been abandoned by his household, as not consenting to their acts.' But this looks like a speculation of the chronicler's. Valence displayed humane consideration for his prisoners, all the more honourable as he had not yet received Edward's letter of 28 June modifying his previous bloodthirsty orders.

After the defeat, Bruce's party broke up into several groups. Sir Simon Fraser was captured at Kirkincliffe near Stirling. Sir Christopher de Seton was taken at Lochore Castle in Fife. The Earl of Lennox made for his own fastnesses. Bruce himself proceeded northwards to Aberdeen. Barbour says he had about 500 followers, the most prominent of whom were his brother Sir Edward, the Earls of Atholl and Errol, Sir William Barondoun, James of Douglas and Sir Nigel Campbell. He kept to high ground, not venturing to the plains, for the population had outwardly passed to the English peace again. Barbour tells pitifully how the fugitives' clothes and shoon were riven and rent before they reached Aberdeen. Here they were met by Nigel Bruce, the queen and other ladies, and here Bruce rested his company 'a good while'.

The English, however, followed up, and Bruce was unable to fight. The whole party, therefore, took to the hills again. The exact date is not recorded, but we know that Valence was at Aberdeen on 3 August. The very next day (4 August), a painful scene was enacted at Newcastle. Fifteen Scots, all prisoners from Methven, including Sir David de Inchmartin, Sir John de Cambhou, Sir John de Somerville, Sir Ralph de Heriz and Sir Alexander Scrymgeour, were arraigned before nine justices whose instructions directed that 'judgment be pronounced as ordained, and none of them be allowed to answer.' They were all hanged. At the same time, John de Seton, who had been taken in Tibbers Castle, which he was holding for Bruce, and who had been present with Bruce at the death of Comyn and at the capture of Dumfries Castle, of which Sir Richard Siward of Tibbers was constable, was condemned, drawn and hanged. It appears to have been as a result of the earnest intervention of Sir Adam de Gordon that Randolph, as we shall henceforth call Thomas Randolph (*Thomas Ranulphi*), Bruce's nephew, later Earl of Moray, was spared.

Bruce and his followers suffered serious hardships in the hill country. Barbour engagingly tells how Douglas especially exerted himself in hunting and fishing and, as became a chivalrous youth, indefatigably served the ladies as well as his lord. The party pushed south-westwards by 'the head of the Tay'. Eventually, they found themselves face to face with the Lord of Lorn, Alexander MacDougall, a 'deadly enemy to the King,' says Barbour, 'for the sake of his uncle John Comyn.' Alexander was really Lord of Argyll and had married Comyn's third daughter. It was his son, John of Lorn, whose uncle Comyn was, and Barbour may mean John. Alexander is said to have had over 1000 men, with the chiefs of Argyll as his lieutenants. Bruce was in no state for battle, but he was encouraged, in his necessity, by the nature of the ground and put on a bold front. A stern combat ensued at Dalry, the 'King's Field', in Strathfillan near Tyndrum. For-

47

dun gives the date 11 August, and, if this is correct, Barbour
has misplaced the episode. The men of Lorn, wielding their
great poleaxes on foot, did serious damage to Bruce's horses
and they wounded badly some of his men, including Douglas and Sir Gilbert de la Haye. Bruce satisfied himself by a
determined charge that further contest would cost him too
many men, and, forming close, he retreated steadily, pro-
tecting his rear in person so vigilantly and boldly that none
of the Lorns dared advance from the main body.

The wrath of Lorn incited two brothers named MacIn-
drosser – that is, sons of Durward (the Doorkeeper) as Barbour explains – to perform an oath they had sworn to slay
Bruce. This oath may possibly be connected with the fact
that Alan Durward, the celebrated Justiciar of Scotland, had
vainly endeavoured to get his family claims to the throne
forwarded by the legitimization of his daughters, his wife
being an illegitimate daughter of Alexander II. Joined by a
third man – possibly the MacKeoch of the Lorn tradition –
they rushed on Bruce in a narrow pass, perhaps between
Loch Dochart and Ben More, where the hill rose so sheer
from the water that he had barely room to turn his horse.
One caught his bridle, but Bruce instantly sheared off his
arm. Another had seized his leg and stirrup, but Bruce rose
in his stirrups and spurred his horse, throwing down his adversary who still grimly maintained his grip. The third
meanwhile had scrambled up the incline and jumped on
Bruce's horse behind him, but Bruce at once dragged him
forward and split his head. He then struck down the man at
his stirrup. This exploit cowed the Lorns. Barbour glorifies
Bruce by citing the admiring comment of MacNaughton, a
Baron of Cowal. 'You seem to enjoy our discomfiture,' said
Lorn angrily. 'No,' replied MacNaughton, 'but never did I

hear tell of such a feat, and one should honour chivalry whether in friend or in foe.' Bruce rode after his men, and Lorn retired in chagrin. Barbour, it will be observed, makes no mention of a personal encounter between Bruce and Lorn, or of the capture of the famous Brooch of Lorn,

> 'Wrought and chased with fair device,
> Studded fair with gems of price.'

Bruce, according to Barbour, now applied himself to rallying the spirits of his party, although probably he was less versed than the devoted archdeacon in historical examples of courage in despair. There was need for encouraging: things were going rapidly from bad to worse. The ladies began to fail. And not only they but some of the men too: the Earl of Atholl, Barbour says, could hold out no longer on any terms. A council of war was called, with the result that Bruce himself, with some 200 of the tougher men, took to the higher hills and Sir Nigel Bruce, taking all the horses, even the king's, led the queen and the other ladies, as well as the more exhausted of the men, back to the Aberdeenshire stronghold of Kildrummy.

Sir Nigel reached Kildrummy in safety. The castle was well provisioned and considered impregnable. It had not been taken by Valence in early August when he 'well settled affairs beyond the Mounth [hills in Deeside], and appointed warders there'. Sir Nigel was soon besieged, probably by the Prince of Wales. A vigorous attack was met by a spirited defence, the besieged frequently sallying forth and fighting at the outworks. There was hardly time for the besiegers to despair of success, as Barbour says they did, when a traitor set fire to the store of corn heaped up in the castle hall, enveloping the place in flames and driving the garrison to the

49

battlements. The English seized their opportunity and attacked as closely as the fire permitted, but they were gallantly repelled. The entrance gate, although burnt, is said to have been so hot that they could not enter. They accordingly waited until morning. The defenders, with great exertion, managed to block up the gate overnight. At daybreak, the attack was renewed with all the energy of certain success. The besieged, however, having neither food nor fuel, recognized that further defence was impossible and surrendered. The precise date is not clear. An anonymous letter dated 13 September states that 'Kildrummy was lately taken by the Prince', but if this date is correct it seems strange that Edward, writing on 22 September, should not say more than that 'all is going well at Kildrummy Castle'.

The prisoners included Sir Nigel Bruce, Sir Robert de Boyd, Sir Alexander de Lindsay 'and other traitors, and many knights and others'. Hemingburgh mentions the queen, but Barbour and Fordun relate that she and the Princess Marjory, in order to escape the siege, had been escorted to the sanctuary of St Duthac at Tain, where they were taken by the Earl of Ross who delivered them to Edward. It may be incidentally noted that some two years afterwards (31 October 1308), the Earl of Ross did fealty and homage to King Robert at Auldearn and was reinstated in his lands.

The fate of the more important prisoners demands particular notice. Most of the captives were interned in English castles, but

> 'Some they ransomed, some they slew,
> And some they hanged, and some they drew.'

The queen was sent to stay at the manor of Burstwick in Holderness, Yorkshire. Edward certainly meant to treat her handsomely. His directions were that she should have 'a waiting-woman and a maidservant, advanced in life, sedate, and of good conversation; a butler, two manservants, and a foot-boy for her chamber, sober and not riotous, to make her bed; three greyhounds, when she inclined to hunt; venison, fish, and the "fairest house in the manor".' Hemingburgh gives two reasons. First, her father, the Red Earl of Ulster, had proved faithful to him. Second, he was pleased with a reported saying of hers on the coronation of her husband. 'Rejoice now, my consort,' Bruce had said, 'for you have been made a Queen, and I a King.'

'I fear, Sir,' she replied, 'we have been made King and Queen after the fashion of children in summer games.'

Other chroniclers give the story with slight variation. In a letter without date but apparently belonging to the next year, she complains to Edward 'that, though he had commanded his bailiffs of Holderness to see herself and her attendants honourably sustained, yet they neither furnish attire for her person or her head, nor a bed, nor furniture of her chambers, saving only a robe of three "garmentz" yearly, and for her servants one robe each for everything'; and she prays him 'to order amendment of her condition, and that her servants be paid for their labour, that she may not be neglected, or that she may have a yearly sum allowed by the King for her maintenance.'

In autumn 1310, she was at Bistelesham; in 1311–12 at Windsor Castle; in autumn 1312 at Shaftesbury; in 1313 at Barking Abbey; in 1313–14 at Rochester Castle; in October 1314 at Carlisle Castle on her way back to Scotland in consequence of Bannockburn.

Marjory, Bruce's daughter, had first been destined for a 'cage' in the Tower of London but was placed by Sir Henry

51

de Percy in the Priory of Watton in Yorkshire. She returned to Scotland with the queen.

Mary Bruce, sister of the king and wife of Sir Nigel Campbell, was kept first in Roxburgh Castle in a 'cage' and then at Newcastle until 25 June 1312, when she was probably exchanged.

Christian Bruce, another sister of the king and widow of Sir Christopher de Seton, was relegated to the Priory of Sixhill in Lincolnshire. She was released on 18 July 1314 and returned with the queen.

The Countess of Buchan was put in a 'cage' in Berwick Castle. The earl, it is said, wanted to kill her, but Edward delivered judgment thus: 'As she did not strike with the sword, she shall not perish by the sword; but, because of the unlawful coronation she performed, let her be closely confined in a stone-and-iron chamber, fashioned in the form of a crown, and suspended at Berwick in the open air outside the castle, so that she may be presented, alive and dead, a spectacle to passers-by and an everlasting reproach.'

In fact, she was placed in a room – or rather an erection of three storeys or rooms – of stout lattice-work in a turret of the castle. She was to be kept so strictly that 'she shall speak to no one, and that neither man nor woman of the nation of Scotland, nor other, shall approach her,' except her keeper and her immediate attendants. The 'cage' was simply an arrangement for 'straiter custody', although rarely judged necessary in the case of ladies. About a year later, the ex-constable of Bristol Castle was reimbursed certain expenditure, part of which was for 'making a wooden cage bound with iron in the said house for the straiter custody of Owen, son of David ap Griffith, a prisoner, shut therein at night.'

A harder fate awaited the foremost knightly defenders of

Kildrummy. Sir Nigel Bruce and several others were drawn, hanged and beheaded at Berwick. The handsome person and gallant bearing of the youthful knight excited general sympathy and regret.

The Earl of Atholl had escaped from Kildrummy and taken to the sea but was driven back by contrary winds and took refuge in a church where he was captured – 'the news whereof eased the King's pain.' At the end of October he was taken to London, tried and condemned. When friends interceded for him and urged his royal blood, 'The higher the rank,' said Edward, 'the worse the fall; hang him higher than the rest.' In virtue of his royal blood he was not drawn, but he was hanged fifty feet high (twenty feet higher than others), taken down half-dead, beheaded and burnt. His head was set on London Bridge, again higher than the rest.

Sir Christopher de Seton had been taken at Lochore (Hemingburgh, Trevet) – if not at Kildrummy (Gray) – betrayed, says Barbour, by MacNab, 'a man of his own household,' 'a disciple of Judas.' 'In hell condemned mot he be!' prays the good archdeacon. He was taken to Dumfries because of the part he had played at the death of Comyn, and there (not, as Barbour says, at London) he was drawn, hanged and beheaded. He was only twenty-eight years old.

Sir Simon Fraser had been captured about 24 August by Sir David de Brechin near Stirling and conducted to London on 6 September. He was tried and condemned, drawn, hanged and beheaded; his body, having been rehung on the gallows for twenty days, was burnt and his head was carried, with the music of horns, to London Bridge and placed near the head of Wallace. Fraser, since turning patriot, had aroused the admiration of foes and friends alike. 'In him,' says Langtoft, 'through his falseness, perished much worth.'

53

'The imprisoned Scots nobles,' says another English chronicler, 'declared he could be neither beaten nor taken, and thought the Scots could not be conquered while he was alive. So much did they believe in him that Sir Herbert de Morham, handsomest and tallest of Scotsmen, a prisoner in the Tower, offered his head to the King to be cut off the day Simon was captured.' Sir Herbert's squire, Thomas du Bois, joined in his master's confident wager. Both of them were beheaded on 7 September, the day after Sir Simon's arrival at the Tower.

But Edward dared not stain his hands with the blood of great churchmen. The Bishops of St Andrews and Glasgow and the Abbot of Scone were conducted to Newcastle-upon-Tyne in the warlike guise in which they are said to have been taken. From Newcastle (10 August) they were led by stages, still traceable, to their separate places of confinement – the castles of Winchester, Porchester and Mere. On the way they were not allowed to communicate with each other or with anyone else 'excepting their keepers only', and on arrival at their several destinations, they were loaded with irons. Edward was keenly anxious to get hold of the Bishop of Moray also, whom he believed – no doubt wrongly – to have been a party to the murder of Comyn but who certainly adhered to Bruce. The bishop, however, had fled to Orkney and for a year left Edward to negotiate with the king of Norway for his surrender.

The Bishop of St Andrews had sagaciously surrendered to Valence four or five days before Methven. He had already (9 June) warmly repudiated the charge of complicity in the death of Comyn. On 9 August, he was severely examined at Newcastle. Why had he concealed his bond with Bruce when he was admitted to the Council at Sheen? He had 'entirely forgotten' it – which is not quite improbable, for, on the face of it at all events, and possibly in fact, it related to the immediate contingencies of eighteen months back. Why did he hasten to Bruce's coronation? He went to see him 'on account of grievous threats against his person and substance, and for no other reason' – but he was not so stiff as the Earl of Strathearn. Neither these nor his further answers are satisfactory. Already he was declaring himself 'heartily sorry'. On 1 June 1308, on an order dated 23 May, he was released from Winchester Castle where he had lain from 24 August 1306, but he was taken bound to remain within the county of Northampton. At Northampton, on 11 August, he swore fealty to Edward in abject terms and vowed to remain within the bounds of the bishopric of Durham. He was creeping northwards. The pope sent a strong remonstrance in his favour, but Edward II had anticipated it by the bishop's release. On 16 February 1310, the bishop figures at the head of a commission of seven, invested, on the urging of the pope, with full powers to treat with Bruce for a cessation of hostilities. On 24 July 1311, he was back in Scotland, and Edward writes to the pope excusing his absence from a General Council held at Vienna on the ground that 'he is much needed to give right direction to the minds of Scotsmen, and in these days no one's exhortations are more readily acquiesced in.' Indeed, 'we have laid upon him various arduous tasks touching the state of the country, and especially its tranquillity.' Besides, 'his absence would be a danger to souls.' In a second letter of excuse, on 4 December, Edward testifies emphatically to his continued fidelity. About two years later, 30 November 1313, the bishop was still so much in favour that Edward dispatched him on an embassy to the king of France. On 25 September 1314, he 'is going abroad on business of his own, by our leave', which implies his final release as a consequence of Bannockburn.

The Bishop of Glasgow was more strictly dealt with. Apparently about the date of his internment in Porchester Castle (say 25 August 1306), he prayed the king, 'for God and for charity and the salvation of his soul, to allow him to remain in England within certain bounds at the King's will, on such surety as the King may demand, till the rising of the Scots be entirely put down.' On 1 December 1308, Edward II delivered him to Arnaud, Bishop of Poitiers, to be taken to the pope, but three days later he wrote to his Holiness and to a number of cardinals that the bishop's crimes forbade any hope that he could be allowed to return to Scotland. He set forth at length the supreme wickedness of the bishop, 'the sower of universal discord', the traitor, the sixfold perjurer, the ecclesiastic taken in arms; 'not a pacific overseer, but a belligerent; not a Levite of the altar, but a horsed warrior, taking to himself a shield for a diocese, a sword for a stole, a corslet for an alb, a helmet for a mitre, a spear for a pastoral staff.' Begging the pope on no account to permit the return of the bishop to Scotland or even 'elsewhere within the King's power', he recommends the appointment of Master Stephen de Segrave, Professor of Canon Law and Dean of Glasgow, to the western bishopric. To the pope the bishop went, and with the pope he apparently remained for two years, for in January 1311, Edward wrote from Berwick to his chancellor informing him that he had heard that the bishop was 'busy suing his deliverance at the Court of Rome' and commanding him 'in concert with the Earl of Lincoln, the Lieutenant and Guardian, and the Treasurer of Scotland, to issue letters under the Great Seal to the Pope, and to the Cardinals named in the enclosed list, urgently opposing the Bishop's restoration either to his office or to his country, and pointing out his evil bearing (*mavoys port*), and his repeated violation of his oath, and anything else likely to induce the Pope to refuse him leave even to return to Scotland.' These representations appear to have stayed the pope's hand, and again, on 23 April, Edward repeated with special urgency his request for the supersession of the bishop by Master Stephen de Segrave. Late in 1313, the bishop was sent back to Edward 'to be detained by the King at pleasure till Scotland was recovered'; and Edward, on 20 November, committed him to the charge of the Prior of Ely, 'to remain at the Priory at his own expenses, and not to go forth except for the purpose of taking the air, under sufficient escort.' On 18 July 1314, Edward ordered him to be brought to York, where he joined Bruce's queen and other Scots prisoners with whom he was sent to Carlisle on 2 October and from there to Scotland. Physically, however, he was worn out; he had become totally blind. He survived his restoration only two years, dying in 1317. It stands to the credit of Bruce that he always retained a strong feeling of gratitude and sympathy for the patriotic, flexible, gallant and much enduring bishop.

The campaign of the east was over. On 4 October 1306, Edward I conferred on Sir Aymer de Valence lands and official honours in the shires of Peebles and Selkirk, and on 7 October he made him keeper of the castle and forest of Jedburgh. On 23 October, Edward received the homage and fealty of James, Steward of Scotland, and restored to him his lands. Of course the English lands and possessions of Bruce and all his adherents were distributed as rewards to the deserving officers and the favourites of the conqueror. The active opposition to the English in Scotland was smothered in blood except in Galloway and Carrick.

CHAPTER V

THE KING IN EXILE

When Sir Nigel Bruce parted for the last time with his brother and passed on his fated way to Kildrummy, the king was left with some two hundred men, all on foot. He kept steadily to the hills where he suffered severely from hunger, cold and wet, until at last he resolved to make southward to Kintyre. Dispatching Sir Nigel Campbell, whose kinsmen dwelt in these parts, to obtain boats and victuals and to meet the party 'at the sea' – either on Loch Long or on the Firth of Clyde – Bruce, says Barbour, struck out for Loch Lomond, probably about Rowardennan. Here he could find no boats, and either way round was long and beset with foes. At last Douglas discovered a sunken boat capable of holding only three men. In the course of a night and a day the party were ferried over, two by two, a few of them, however, swimming 'with fardel on back'. Meanwhile Bruce cheered their drooping spirits by reading from the old romance how Fierabras was overcome by the right doughty Oliver and how the Twelve (Eleven) Peers held out in Aigremont against Lawyne (Laban, Balan) until they were delivered by Charlemagne.

The most pressing difficulty was lack of food. Presently, however, this was relieved by the Earl of Lennox who had noted the sound of the king's horn and joyfully hastened to

58

him. Shortly Sir Nigel returned with boats and food in abundance. Bruce and his friends embarked. Barbour has a dramatic story how Lennox made delay in starting, how his boat was pursued, probably by Lorn's men, and how he escaped by throwing overboard his belongings which the enemy stopped to appropriate. The boats ran down the Firth and safely landed the party in Kintyre.

Here Bruce received a friendly welcome from Angus of Islay, Lord of Kintyre, who placed at his disposal the rock fortress of Dunaverty. He entertained suspicions of treachery, however, and stayed only three days. Then, with all his followers, he passed over to the island of Rathlin, off the coast of Ireland, an exile from his kingdom.

Such is Barbour's story. Taking it, meantime, as it stands, let us see what the English had been doing in the southwest. The details of operations are very scanty. Percy, the king's lieutenant on the western March, had exerted himself during June, July and August in fortifying and provisioning the castles. Lochmaben Castle fell on 11 July, and Prince Edward felt himself free to go to Valence at Perth a few days later and to carry through the siege of Kildrummy by the middle of September. He seems to have acted with more zeal than prudence. Rishanger says he took 'such vengeance that he spared neither sex nor age; towns, too, and hamlets, wherever he came he set on fire, and he mercilessly devastated the country.' This conduct 'is said to have gravely displeased the King his father, who chid him severely.' The king had moved northwards by slow stages, borne in a litter on horseback. It was 29 September when he reached the priory of Lanercost, eight miles from Carlisle, and this house he made his headquarters until 26 March.

In September, the siege of Dunaverty was proceeding un-

der the direction of Sir John Botetourte, the king's ablest engineer. The local people were very slack in aiding the English, and Edward, on 25 September, ordered Sir John de
Menteith to compel them to supply the besiegers with provisions and necessaries, 'if they will not with a good grace'.
The next month Edward empowered Sir John of Argyll to
receive to his peace, on special conditions, Donald of Islay,
Gotheri, his brother, John MacNakyld and Sir Patrick de
Graham. The conditions suggest that they had been in a position to drive a good bargain, and the submission of the first
three at least may perhaps be connected with the capitula-
tion of Dunaverty towards the end of October.

Now, at what date did Bruce go from Dunaverty to Rathlin? Even were it not for Barbour's weather indications
and for the necessity of the awkward admission that, for
some good reason – say food supplies – Bruce fled before
the English approach and left some of his staunchest supporters in Dunaverty, it is difficult to suppose that he
could have stayed undisturbed in Rathlin from mid-September to the end of January. Sir Thomas Gray records
that Prince Edward, on his return from Kildrummy (say
mid-September), had an interview with Bruce, 'who had
re-entered from the Isles and had collected a force in
Atholl', at the bridge of Perth, much to the displeasure of
the king his father. Gray is manifestly wrong in some
points, and he may be wrong in all. Still, Bruce, finding his
way barred by Alexander of Argyll and not daring to de-
scend to the plains, may likely enough have turned back to
Atholl and, on hearing of the disaster of Kildrummy and the
capture of his queen, his daughter and his sisters, may have
felt driven to a desperate attempt at reaching an accommodation. On such a supposition, it becomes easy to ac-

cept Barbour's Perthshire and Atlantic weather to absolve
Bruce from an apparent sacrifice of friends in Dunaverty
and to shorten to a credible length his stay on Rathlin.
There are two difficulties to this view. One is that the
English should have gone so far out of their way as to besiege Dunaverty so zealously or at all. They seem, however,
to have been under the impression that Bruce himself was
there. The other difficulty is that Dunaverty had just been
taken by the English. But if the astute Angus Oig was
governor when Bruce arrived, Dunaverty was remote
enough to allow him large scope for temporizing.

The secret of Bruce's retreat appears to have been well
kept. In October, indeed, Edward had commissioned Sir
John of Argyll admiral on the west coast. But he did not find
Bruce. It was not until 29 January that Edward commanded
the Treasurer of Ireland to aid Sir Hugh Bisset in fitting out
'as many well-manned vessels as he can procure, to come to
the Isles and the Scottish coast, and join Sir John de Menteith in putting down Robert de Bruce and his accomplices
lurking there, and in cutting off their retreat.' More precise
are the terms of appointment of Sir Simon de Montacute
(30 January) as commander of the fleet specially destined 'for
service against the rebels lurking in Scotland, and in the Isles
between Scotland and Ireland.' On 1 February, Edward ordered up vessels from Skinburness and neighbouring ports
'towards Ayr in pursuit of Robert de Bruce and his abettors,
and to cut off his retreat.' Bruce, therefore, must have left
Rathlin some days before the end of January, probably because of the menace of the English fleet.

Barbour keeps him in Rathlin until winter was nearly
gone – not really an inconsistency – but he seems to attribute the exodus to Douglas's chafing at inaction. Douglas,

he says, proposed to Boyd an attempt on Brodick Castle, which Boyd knew well. With Bruce's leave they proceeded to Arran and overnight set ambush at the castle. As they lay in wait, the sub-warden arrived with over thirty men in three boats, bringing provisions and arms, and Douglas and Boyd set upon them. The outcry brought men from the castle, who fled, however, before the bold advance of the Scots and barred the gate. The Scots appropriated the sub-warden's provisions and arms and took up a position in a narrow pass, and the garrison does not seem to have even attempted to dislodge them.

On the tenth day, it is said, Bruce arrived with the rest of his men in thirty-three small boats and was conducted by a woman to the glen where Douglas and Boyd were, strangely ignorant of his coming. Then Bruce determined to dispatch the trusty Cuthbert of Carrick to sound out the people on the mainland, arranging that Cuthbert, in case he found them favourable, should raise a fire on Turnberry Point at a fixed time. Cuthbert found Percy in Turnberry Castle with some 300 men. As for the Scots, some were willing, but afraid, while most were distinctly hostile. He dared not fire the beacon.

At the appointed time, Bruce looked eagerly for the signal. He saw a fire. The party put to sea, 300 strong, and rowed in the dusk and the dark direct to the fire. Cuthbert was at his wits' end; he dared not extinguish the fire. He met Bruce at the shore and explained the uncertain attitude of the people. 'Why, then,' demanded Bruce angrily, with a suspicion of treachery, 'why did you light the fire?' Cuthbert explained it was none of his doing and beyond his help. What was to be done? A council of war was held. Sir Edward Bruce is said to have decided the question by a point-blank refusal to retire. He, for one, would strike at once, come what might.

Cuthbert had learned that two-thirds of the garrison were lodged in the town. Bruce and his men entered quietly in small parties, breaking open the doors and slaying all they found. Percy did not venture to sally from the castle. Bruce stayed three days, testing the feeling of the people, but even those who secretly favoured him were afraid to show an open preference. It is said that a lady, a near relative of his own, Christian of the Isles, came and encouraged him and afterwards sent him frequent supplies of money and food. While confining Percy, he harried the country with increasing daring. A strong force of Northumberland men, however, raised the siege. Hemingburgh places Bruce's attack on Turnberry Castle 'about Michaelmas', but it seems very unlikely that Bruce ventured to take the field in the southwest before he went to Rathlin.

Apart from Barbour's details, it is plain that Bruce had struck a heavy blow. On 6 February, Edward wrote to his treasurer expressing surprise 'at having no news of Valence and his forces since he went to Ayr, if they have done any exploit or pursued the enemy.' He commands him 'quickly to order Valence, Percy, and Sir John de St John, and others he sees, to send a trustworthy man without delay with full particulars of their doings and the state of affairs.' And he is 'not to forget in his letter to them to say on the King's behalf that he hears they have done so badly that they do not wish him to know.' To the same effect he wrote himself to Valence on 11 February and commanded him 'to write distinctly and clearly by the bearer the news of the parts where he is, the state of affairs there, and the doings of himself and the others hitherto, and how he and they have arranged further proceedings. For he suspects from his silence that he has so over-cautiously conducted matters that he wishes to conceal his actions.' At the same time he addressed similar letters to the Earls of Gloucester and Hereford, St John and Percy. The tone is too earnest to permit the supposition that Edward was dissembling knowledge of the facts.

Bruce had at last regained a footing, although but precarious footing, in his kingdom and rendered Edward anxious about the immediate future.

CHAPTER VI

THE TURN OF THE TIDE

In the midst of his new success, another severe family blow was impending on Bruce. On 10 February 1307 – the first anniversary of the Dumfries tragedy – his brothers, Thomas and Alexander, made a raid on Galloway with some 300 Scots and 700 Irish auxiliaries, landing at Loch Ryan, in the territory of Sir Dougal MacDowall. In a desperate fight, the force was completely crushed by MacDowall who captured Thomas and Alexander and Sir Reginald Crawford, Wallace's uncle, all 'wounded and half-dead'. Hemingburgh says the Scots were caught by surprise. Trevet adds 'in the night'. MacDowall delivered his chief prisoners, together with the heads of a baron of Kintyre and two Irish kinglets, to Prince Edward at Wetheral, near Carlisle. These prisoners were all executed at Carlisle on 17 February. Sir Thomas Bruce was drawn, hanged and beheaded; Alexander Bruce, being a clergyman (Dean of Glasgow), was not drawn but he and Sir Reginald Crawford, and apparently Sir Brice de Blair, were hanged and beheaded. Thomas's head was placed on the castle tower, and the heads of the others graced the three gates of the city. MacDowall was rewarded with the lands and possessions of Sir Robert de Boyd and Sir Brice de Blair, and on 19 February, he received fifty marks and a charger, while on 1 March a profitable privilege was conferred, at his instance, upon his son.

According to Gray and Trevet, Bruce had sent his brothers to Nithsdale and Annandale 'to gain over the people'. It may be that the expedition was intended first to operate as a diversion and then to join Bruce himself in Nithsdale. For Bruce, if not already in these parts, was moving there. On 12 February Sir John Botetourte, with a considerable force, including over a score of knights, started to make a raid on Bruce in Nithsdale, and on 8 March he was reinforced by 180 archers from Carlisle. The details, however, are not recorded.

It was probably in February, upon the landing of Bruce in Carrick, that Edward issued from Lanercost an ordinance intended to conciliate the Scots while it graded carefully the degrees of punishment for the worst classes of delinquents. Contrary to the king's intention, the ordinance had been interpreted as too harsh and rigorous. On 13 March, therefore, he materially modified it. A few days later he directed steps to be taken for the repair and fortification of several castles on the east side beyond Forth and ordered fresh levies from the northern counties of England to muster, 2300 strong, at Carlisle by a fortnight after Easter.

In a lull in the Nithsdale operations, Bruce is said to have reluctantly granted Douglas leave to go to Douglasdale, accompanied only by two yeomen. On arrival, Douglas disclosed himself to Tom Dickson of Hazelside, a staunch old warrior-tenant of his father's, who was overjoyed to see the youth and introduced him to the other loyal men of the land, one by one, at private conferences. It was quickly decided to attack the unsuspecting garrison of Douglas Castle in St Bride's Church on Palm Sunday (19 March). The countrymen would bring concealed weapons, and Douglas would appear with his two men in the guise of a corn-thresher, a threadbare mantle on his back and a flail on his shoulder. The moment he raised his war cry, they would overpower the soldiers and then the castle would offer no resistance.

Everything went as planned except that an overeager friend prematurely raised the Douglas war cry. Dickson instantly fell upon the English in the chancel and a neighbour followed his example, but both were slain. At this moment Douglas came on the scene, raised his war cry and pressed hard on the English who manfully defended themselves. About twenty were killed; the remaining ten were taken prisoners. At the castle, Douglas found only the porter and the cook, and so he barred the gates and dined at leisure. After dinner, he packed up valuables, arms and other portable things and proceeded to destroy what he could not take away. He piled the wheat, flour, meal and malt on the floor of the wine cellar, beheaded the prisoners on the pile and broached the wine casks. This ghastly mess was locally designated 'the Douglas Larder'. He then spoilt the well by throwing in salt and dead horses. Finally, he set fire to the castle and left nothing but stones. The party dispersed and hid away their wounded. But Clifford, for whom the castle had been held, soon had it rebuilt and regarrisoned.

A later petition by Lucas de Barry says that Lucas had been 'under Sir Robert de Clifford in Douglas Castle when Sir Robert de Brus and Sir James Douglas attacked it, the year when the late King died.' But this does not necessarily mean that either Clifford or Bruce was there in person.

On the same Sunday morning, Edward entered Carlisle with Peter, Cardinal Bishop of St Sabine, a papal legate who had just arrived to arrange terms of peace between the English and French kings on the basis of a marriage between

Prince Edward and Isabella, daughter of the king of France. On the Wednesday following, in the cathedral, the legate explained the objects of his mission and, with bell, book and candle, excommunicated the murderers of Comyn, with all their aiders and abettors. The like denunciation was busily repeated throughout the churches, especially of the north of England. On Friday, the peace was proclaimed.

Towards the end of March, Sir John Wallace is said to have been captured 'in the plain, pursued by the northerners' and was taken to Carlisle. Edward sent him to London, 'fettered on a hackney', to undergo the same barbarous death as his heroic brother. His head was fixed on London Bridge, 'raised with shouts,' says Langtoft, 'near the head of his brother, William the Wicked.' It could not have been more nobly honoured.

By the middle of April, Bruce had moved to Glen Trool where he was hard beset for some three weeks by superior forces under a number of able knights, young Sir John Comyn among them. The incidents of the period have not been preserved. Barbour, indeed, tells how Valence and Clifford advanced stealthily on Bruce with over 1500 against fewer than 300 men and found him in a narrow pass where horse could not reach him. Valence sent a woman disguised as a beggar to spy out the position, but Bruce saw through the dodge and the spy confessed. The English had to advance on foot. Bruce dashed upon them with fury, seizing with his own hand their foremost banner. Some of his men, Barbour admits, had gone off but came back on seeing how the fight went. The foremost English company being overpowered, the main body retreated, and a quarrel between Clifford and Vaux seems to point to a fruitless attempt of Clifford's to rally the fugitives. One can only say that some such incidents are probable enough. Anyhow, Bruce appears to have baffled all the attempts of the English in Glen Trool and to have got away towards Lothian.

In Lothian, Bruce found friends. The people, Hemingburgh explains, had been exasperated during the preceding year by the justice of the English justiciars and therefore, 'as if unanimously, they rose and went with Bruce, willing rather to die than to be judged by the English laws.' Thus reinforced, Bruce turned back to meet Valence. Perhaps it was now that he overran Kyle and Cunningham. Valence, says Barbour, dispatched from Bothwell 1000 men under Sir Philip de Mowbray whom Douglas with 60 men met at Ederford, a narrow pass between two marshes, and by skilful strategy totally defeated. Stung by this ignominious reverse, Valence challenged Bruce, who lay at Galston, to meet him on 10 May at Loudon Hill – the scene of Wallace's father's death and of Wallace's first victory. Bruce accepted the challenge. Choosing his ground between two stretches of moss, he cut three deep trenches (with adequate gaps for the passage of his men) across the hard moor between and marshalled his 600 followers so that Valence's 3000 men could come into action only in detail. He ordered a fierce onset on the foremost with a view to discouraging the rest – the successful tactic in Glen Trool – and Sir Edward and Douglas, as well as himself, are said to have performed prodigious feats of valour. The English gave way, and Valence was driven from the field. Barbour says he retreated to Bothwell; Gray states that Bruce pursued him to Ayr. Three days later, Bruce also defeated the Earl of Gloucester with even greater slaughter (says Hemingburgh) than had reddened Loudon Hill and besieged him in Ayr Castle.

From an anonymous letter dated 15 May, we learn without surprise that Edward 'was much enraged that the Warden and his force had retreated before King Hobbe' – his familiar designation of Bruce. What does surprise one is to learn, on the same authority, that 'James of Douglas sent and begged to be received, but, when he saw the King's forces retreat, he drew back.' It would be quite understandable that the hardships of his first terrible year of service had shaken the nerve of the youthful warrior. But there were now 'rumours of treasonable dealings between some of the English and the enemy', and it seems far more probable that Douglas was engineering one of his ruses. It needs better evidence to stamp this solitary suggestion of a blot on the clear escutcheon of Douglas.

The news of Bruce's success, no doubt exaggerated and distorted, produced a great sensation in the northern parts of Scotland. An anonymous letter, written from Forfar to some high official under the date of 15 May, graphically pictures the local feeling.

'The writer hears that Sir Robert de Brus never had the goodwill of his own followers or the people at large, or even half of them, so much with him as now; and it now first appears that he was right, and God is openly with him, as he has destroyed all the King's power both among the English and the Scots, and the English force is in retreat to its own country not to return. And they firmly believe, by the encouragement of the false preachers who come from the host, that Sir Robert de Brus will now have his will. And these preachers are such as have been attached before the Warden and the justices as abettors of war, and are at present freed on guarantees and deceiving the people thus by their false preachment. For he [the writer] believes assuredly, as he hears from Sir Reginald de Cheyne, Sir Duncan de Frendraught, and Sir Gilbert de Glencairney, and others who watch the peace both beyond and on this side of the mountains

(Mounth), that, if Sir Robert de Brus can escape any way 'saun dreytes 'or towards the parts of Ross, he will find them all ready at his will more entirely than ever, unless the King will be pleased to send more men-at-arms to these parts; for there are many people living well and loyally at his faith provided the English are in power, otherwise they see that they must be at the enemies' will through default of the King and his Council, as they say. And it would be a deadly sin to leave them so without protection among enemies. And may it please God to keep the King's life, for when we lose him, which God forbid, say they openly, all must be on one side, or they must die or leave the country with all those who love the King, if other counsel or aid be not sent them. For these preachers have told them that they have found a prophecy of Merlin, how, after the death of the grasping King (*le Roi Coueytous*), the Scottish people and the Bretons shall league together, and have the sovereign hand and their will, and live together in accord till the end of the world.'

It was probably reports of this tenor that drew Valence and Bevercotes on a hasty visit to the north immediately after Loudon Hill. They were both in Inverness on 20 May.

The reverses sustained by Valence and Gloucester led to increased activity on the English side. The Bishop of Chester, with his successor as treasurer (the Bishop of Lichfield and Coventry), was at Lanark on 15 May, at Dumfries the next day and on 18 May he was back at Carlisle, having seen to the provisioning of the fortresses. Edward was 'so greatly pleased with his account that he kissed him – especially for his borrowing the castle of Cumnock from its owner, Earl Patrick, for a term, and garrisoning it with 30 men-at-arms under Sir Ingram de Umfraville and Sir William de Felton, besides 100 foot.' The bishop went south next day to represent Edward at the funeral of the Countess of Gloucester, the king's daughter Joan.

Edward himself was too ill to travel. Besides, he was immersed in military preparations, summoning reinforcements and hurrying up supplies. Bruce, although unable to maintain the siege of Ayr, did considerable damage, for on 1 June, Valence requisitioned masons and carpenters from Carlisle 'to repair the castle and houses'. At the same time, Valence added some 300 men to the garrison 'to strengthen the castle and secure the country round, while he is on his foray towards Carrick and Glen Trool.' He was following up Bruce. Probably, too, he avenged Loudon Hill before the arrival of Edward's fresh levies which had been summoned to be at Carlisle by the middle of July. Hemingburgh says the English 'defeated Bruce with great slaughter, so that he lurked thereafter in moors and marshes' with the ridiculous force of 'some 10,000 foot, and the English could not get at him, as he always slipped out of their hands.' Gray says that Bruce was so badly beaten 'that he retired on foot through the mountains, and from isle to isle, and sometimes he had not so much as a single companion with him.' One is inclined to give the credit of this defeat to Valence – if defeat there was. Bruce may have taken refuge again in Glen Trool; Gray's mention of the isles may result from a confusion with earlier events. This record of fresh disaster finds no mention in Barbour or in Fordun.

Sir Thomas Gray, professing to quote from 'the chronicles of his deeds', relates how at this time Bruce came, all alone, to a passage between two islands, over which he was ferried by two boatmen. Had he heard any news of what had become of Bruce? they asked. 'None,' he replied. 'Certes,' said they, 'we would we had grip of him at this moment; he should die by our hands.' 'And why?' queried Bruce. 'Because he murdered John Comyn, our lord,' was the answer.

They landed him. 'My good fellows,' said Bruce, 'you wanted to get hold of Robert de Bruce. Look at me! – that will give you satisfaction. And were it not that you have done me the courtesy of ferrying me over this narrow passage, you should rue your wish.' So he went on his way.

Barbour recounts various exploits of Bruce and Douglas between the landing in Carrick and the first retreat to Glen Trool, but if they represent facts they must clearly be spread over a longer period.

For example. Sir Ingram Bell, the governor of Ayr – Barbour writes Sir Ingram de Umfraville, who was probably in Cumnock Castle – intrigued with a personal attendant of Bruce's, a man of local importance, a one-eyed, sturdy rascal closely related to Bruce. The villain was promised a reward of £40 in land to plot the king's death. With his two sons, who were also trusted by Bruce, he lay in wait one morning for his master when he had gone out with only a page in attendance. Bruce, suspecting the men, ordered them to stand. As they still came on, he drew his page's bow and shot the father in the eye and with his sword he split the skull of one son after the other. This may be one of half a dozen possible variants of the story of the Brooch of Lorn.

Not long afterwards, in the dusk of evening, Bruce with 60 men was attacked by over 200 Galwegians who had brought a sleuthhound to track him. Warned by his sentinels, he drew his men into a narrow pass in a bog, and leaving Sir Gilbert de la Haye in charge went out with two men to reconnoitre the position. Passing some way along the water side, he found the banks high and the water deep, and no ford except the one he had crossed. Here he sent his men back to camp and watched alone. Presently he heard the deep baying of the hound and soon the enemy appeared under a bright moon. He determined to stand; they must come on singly in the strait passage. They plunged confidently into the water, but Bruce bore down the foremost with his spear and stabbed the horse, which fell in the ascent from the water and impeded the others. He kept the ford, and when his men came up they found fourteen slain and the rest in retreat. The rumour of this exploit drew many to his side.

Again Douglas repaired to Douglasdale and set an ambush near Sandilands. With a small party he then took some from cattle near the castle of Douglas and drove them off. Thirlwall, the constable, sallied out and pursued the party past the ambush. Attacked suddenly, he was slain in attempted defence together with most of his men. The survivors fled to the castle, barred the gate and manned the walls. Douglas had to content himself with what booty he could find around the castle.

Presently Douglas, hearing of the approach of Valence with a strong force, joined the king in a narrow pass near Cumnock. Bruce had only 300 men. Valence was accompanied by John of Lorn who headed over 800 and had a sleuthhound said to have once been a favourite of Bruce's. On finding himself caught between the two bodies, Bruce divided his men into three companies, anticipating that the enemy would follow his own track, so his other two companies would escape. The hound followed Bruce, who gradually dispersed his company, at last keeping only his foster brother with him. Still the hound persisted. John of Lorn then sent forward five of his stoutest men to take Bruce. Three attacked Bruce, two assailed his foster brother. Bruce killed one of his opponents and, marking the dismay of the others, jumped aside to help his foster brother and struck off the head of one of his assailants. He then killed his own two pursuers while his foster brother dispatched the only one remaining. Meantime Lorn closed up with the hound. Bruce, with his companion, made for a wood and threw himself down by a stream, declaring he could go no farther, but yielding to his friend's remonstrances, he got up, and they waded together some way down the stream, thus baffling the hound and escaping further pursuit. Another account, according to Barbour, was that the king's companion lurked in a thicket and shot the hound with an arrow. Anyhow, Bruce escaped. It is said that Randolph captured Bruce's banner in the pursuit, much to the satisfaction of the English king.

Having got clear of the forest, Bruce and his companion were crossing a moor when they came on three men armed with swords and axes, one of them carrying a sheep on his shoulder. The men said they wished to join Bruce, and Bruce said he would take them to him. They realized that he was Bruce, and he realized that they were enemies. Bruce insisted that until better acquainted they should travel separately and in front of him. Coming to an empty house at night, they killed the sheep, roasted it, divided it and dined at opposite ends of the room. Bruce, tired and hungry as he had been, must sleep, his man promising to keep watch. His man, however, fell asleep too; he 'might not hold up an e'e'. The men then attacked Bruce who instantly awoke, grasped his sword and trod heavily on his man. Bruce slew the three but lost his companion who was killed in his sleep.

Bruce now made for the rallying point of his dispersed companies. Here he found the mistress of the house 'sitting on a bink' (bench). In answer to her exhaustive inquiries, he said he was a wayfarer. 'All wayfarers,' said she, 'are welcome for the sake of one – King Robert the Bruce.' Then the king revealed himself. Where were his men? she asked.

He had none. Thereupon the gallant woman declared her two big sons should become his men. As he sat to eat, he heard the tread of soldiers and started up to defend himself. It was Douglas and Sir Edward Bruce with 150 men.

Bruce now suggested that the enemy, confident that his force was dissipated, would be open to surprise. He made a forced march overnight and at daylight caught a large detachment – certainly nothing like 2000 (Barbour's figure) – in some town and slew two-thirds of them. He retreated before the main body began to stir, and Valence did not pursue.

On another occasion Bruce went hunting alone, with two hounds. He had his sword but had laid aside his armour. Presently he saw three men with bows approaching – men who had in fact been watching for such an opportunity to take vengeance for Comyn. Bruce taunted them for attacking with arrows, three to one, and they chivalrously threw down their bows and drew their swords. Bruce struck down one; a hound fastened on another's throat and brought him to the ground, when Bruce cut his back in two, and the third, fleeing to the wood, was seized and pulled down by the other hound and dispatched by Bruce.

These stories represent early traditions and may easily be true, although they may be merely imaginary. The three-men stories may be variants of a single original but by no means necessarily.

On 7 July 1307, Edward I died at Burgh-on-Sands, some three miles from Carlisle. Because of the poor success of his lieutenants, the gallant king had determined to move forward in person. On Monday 3 July, he is said to have advanced from Carlisle, but it was Thursday before he reached

Burgh-on-Sands. On Friday, as his attendants raised him up in bed to eat, he died in their hands. On his sickbed – or, as Walsingham says, on his deathbed – Edward had again charged the prince to persist steadily in the war against Bruce, taking his bones with him in a casket. 'For,' said the dying king with heroic confidence, 'no one will be able to overcome you while you have my bones borne with you.' But all his dying advice and solemn charges the prince eventually disregarded.

The body of the late king was conveyed south in great state to lie in the church at Waltham until a definite settlement was attained in Scotland. The prince attended the cortege for several stages and then returned to Carlisle. Edward was buried at Westminster on 28 October.

Edward I was not only the greatest of English kings but one of the greatest of Englishmen. His treatment of Scotland, however he may have reasoned out the justice of it, must always remain a very dark blot on his memory. Never was his military ardour or his personal resolution more signally manifested than in the last months and days of his latest expedition. He died in harness, his valiant spirit shining undimmed until the moment it was quenched by death itself. The virile judgment and stern purpose of Edward I was succeeded by the childish incompetence and obstinacy of Edward II. The death of the great king assured the eventual triumph of Bruce. The moment anticipated by nationalists with hope and by anti-nationalists with dread had come. It was the turn of the tide.

CHAPTER VII

*R*ECONQUEST OF TERRITORY

While the great Edward was passing south on his last march, Valence was actively engaged in strengthening the English positions in Kyle and Carrick. Percy held Ayr Castle and John of Argyll guarded Ayr town and neighbourhood with a large force that was presently joined by half a score of redoubtable Scots knights with their followings.

The young king started from Carlisle on 31 July 1307 for Dumfries where many Scots nobles obeyed his summons to do homage and fealty. Advancing up the valley of the Nith, he was at Cumnock on 21 August and stayed there fully a week. At Tinwald, on 30 August, he confirmed Valence in the office of Warden of Scotland. He offered to receive to his peace all Scotsmen not implicated in the murder of Comyn. The Lanercost chronicler says he divided his army into three bodies to pursue Bruce, but the pursuit was unsuccessful, and on 4 September he returned to Carlisle with empty hands.

The effects of the accession of Edward II were quickly apparent. No sooner had he retired than the whole Border was ablaze. Even the faithful men of Selkirk and Tweeddale and of the Forest, tenants of the warden himself, rose in force, and on 12 September the Sheriff of Roxburgh reported that 'the poor tenants' of his district had fled into England with their goods for fear of the enemy. The weight of the Scots attack, however, was thrown upon Galloway and the Mac-Dowalls. The English settlers fled in great numbers, for on 25 September, Edward ordered Clifford, the justiciar of the forest beyond Trent, 'to allow the men of Galloway to feed their flocks and herds in Englewood Forest, whither they have come to take refuge for fear of Robert de Brus and his accomplices.' On the same day he directed Sir Thomas de Multon of Egremont and four other northern barons to hasten to Lancashire, Cumberland and Westmorland to assist John, Baron of Wigton, and Richard le Brun, his justices there, 'for the salvation and quiet of the men of those parts', and to redress the wrongs and losses they sustained and to repel the incursions of the Scots. It looks as if a swift foray had been executed by the men of Selkirk and Tweeddale.

On 30 September, Edward, who had now learned further from St John, MacDowall and other officers in Galloway, that Bruce was 'burning and plundering, and inciting and compelling the inhabitants to rebel', commanded Sir John de Bretagne, who had just succeeded Valence, to march against the enemy. At the same time he summoned to the warden's assistance Earl Patrick and half a dozen other powerful Scots as well as the Baron of Wigton and Richard le Brun, apparently already relieved of their Selkirk visitors and the keepers of the peace of Northumberland and Tyndale. The Lanercost chronicler admits that the Galwegians purchased peace, being unable to resist the forces of Bruce.

Sir Thomas Gray also bears testimony to Bruce's activity and explains the favour he steadily gained, in part at least, by the harsh conduct of English officials 'for purposes of indi-

79

vidual advantage.' We have already seen that as early as May Scotland beyond the Forth was ready for the advent of Bruce, and the English officers were looking forward with dread to the death of Edward I. And now Bruce turned from Galloway to the north.

According to Fordun, Bruce advanced as far as Inverness, where he took the castle and levelled it to the ground, slaying the garrison. The other fortresses of the north he dealt with in the same drastic way. It was in this expedition, no doubt, in late October and November 1307 that Bruce overran Ross, Sutherland and Caithness and compelled the Earl of Ross to take truce. The earl's apologetic petition to Edward explains how Bruce came against him with 3000 men and subjugated these counties 'and would have destroyed them utterly if we had not taken truce with him at the entreaty of the good people both religious and other, till Whitsunday next.' Ross declares that he could get no help from the Warden of Moray. The Bishop of Moray, who had taken refuge in Orkney for about a year and whose lands had been loyally raided by Ross, had by this time returned to Edward's peace and was demanding damages for the wasting of his lands. He, at any rate, was not likely to have moved a finger against Bruce; on the contrary, he no doubt privately aided him. Ross's apologies were accepted, for in May 1308 he appears as lieutenant of the Warden of Scotland and is requested to remain in office until midsummer. But on 31 October, he submitted to Bruce, who reinstated him in his lands (with fresh additions), and his name heads the roll of Bruce's parliament at St Andrews on 16 March 1309.

Barbour, making no mention of these exploits, brings Bruce north of the Mounth hills of Deeside and on to Inverurie in Aberdeenshire. Bruce is joined by Sir Alexander Fraser and Simon Fraser, the famous Sir Simon's brother and son, who had apparently been acting in his interests in the north, opposed mainly by Comyn (Earl of Buchan), Sir John de Mowbray and Sir David de Brechin.

At Inverurie Bruce fell very sick. He could neither eat nor drink; no medicine did him any good; he became too weak to ride or to walk. Sir Edward Bruce, says Barbour, tried to comfort the men, but it seems much more likely that Sir Edward remained in command in Galloway while Douglas made excursions towards the eastern border. At any rate, Bruce's men would not fight while their chief was ill, or Bruce had too much prudence to allow them, so they placed him on a litter and carried him into the Slevach (mountain fastnesses). Comyn, hearing of Bruce's serious illness, advanced against him with Mowbray and Brechin and with a largely superior force. The time, says Barbour, was 'after Martinmas, when snow covered all the land.' Bruce quietly awaited attack. On three successive days there occurred skirmishes between bodies of archers, Buchan's men getting the worst of the encounter day after day. Buchan's force, however, was continuously obtaining additions while Bruce was getting pinched with hunger. Placing the king in his litter again, Bruce's men changed quarters, marching slowly in fighting order with their sick chief in the centre and restricting themselves rigidly to defence. They took up a position in Strathbogie, a little farther north, and Buchan's force abandoned the pursuit and dispersed.

The king gradually regained strength and returned to Inverurie 'to be in the plains for the winter' for the better chances of food. Again Buchan proceeded to attack him, reaching Oldmeldrum 'on the evening before Yule even' (4

January) 1308, with about 1000 men. Next day Brechin made a dash at Inverurie, whereupon Bruce, in spite of re- monstrances, determined to mount and fight, although, says . Fordun, 'he could not go upright, but with the help of two men to prop him up'. He is said to have had 'near 700 men'. He advanced towards Oldmeldrum and, as the enemy re- treated, pressed steadily upon them, pushing their retreat into flight and pursuing them, Fordun says, as far as Fyvie. Buchan and Mowbray fled to England, while Brechin stood a siege in his own castle of Brechin. Bruce's 'herschip' (har- rying) of the district of Buchan is said to have been so exem- plary that men lamented it for half a century afterwards.

There are discrepancies between Barbour's account and Fordun's. Fordun dates Buchan's retirement from the Slevach on Christmas Day (on which Barbour fights at Inverurie and Oldmeldrum), and he arranges a truce on the occasion. It is in the Slevach, he says, that Bruce's illness be- gins. He dates the battle of Inverurie, without mention of Oldmeldrum, vaguely in 1308. He also calls Mowbray Philip, not John, and he says nothing of Brechin. Buchan and Mowbray, if they did not then flee to England, at any rate went south not very long after this time, and if Brechin surrendered his castle, it was certainly not, as Barbour says it was, to David, Earl of Atholl, who was on the English side. On 20 May 1308, Edward writes to thank a great number of his officers in Scotland, including Atholl, Buchan, Brechin, John de Mowbray and others, for their faithful service, and he requests Buchan to remain 'in the district committed to him' until 1 August. This may mean that up to May he had remained in command in the north, although keeping clear of Bruce's devastating track.

Having reduced the country beyond the Grampians ('be-north the Mounth'), Bruce descended upon Angus. Barbour says nothing of an attack on Brechin Castle, having already recorded its capture and the submission of Sir David to Bruce. But, as we have seen, Sir David was still, and indeed, for several years to come, on the English side, and Barbour was evidently misinformed. Forfar Castle was taken by Philip the Forester of Platter; the watch had not been vigilant and Philip scaled the walls. Bruce demolished the castle, either because it was of the old ineffective type or because he had no means of holding it. He then, according to Barbour, besieged Perth, which was strongly fortified and was held by Moffat and Oliphant – Sir William Oliphant, the gallant defender of Stirling who had been released from the Tower on 24 May 1308, having lain rusting there for nearly four years. The Earl of Strathearn, says Barbour, was also in the garrison, while his son and his men were in Bruce's camp. But Barbour is mistaken, for although Strathearn had been transferred from Rochester Castle to York Castle in the preceding November, he does not appear to have been released until 18 November of this year.

Frequent skirmishes took place during a six weeks' siege, when Bruce suddenly decamped amid the premature jeers of the garrison. After eight days he returned suddenly in the night and, finding the English lulled into security, plunged into the moat up to his neck, mounted the walls by ladder and surprised the sentinels. His men, dispersed in groups, gave the garrison no chance to marshal for effective defence. The English leaders were taken but few men were slain in consideration of their decent treatment of Scots. There was much booty for the victors. Bruce demolished the walls and the towers. 'Was none that durst him then withstand.' Whether this capture of Perth is fact or not – and probably it should be placed at a later date – Bruce now had the upper hand north of Forth.

While Bruce was reconquering his kingdom in the north, Edward II had married Isabella of France at Boulogne on 28 January 1308 and had been crowned at Westminster on 25 February. He had at once plunged himself into difficulties with his barons by his infatuation for Piers de Gaveston. In June some purpose of accommodation with Bruce appears to have been pressed upon the English king. There exists a memorandum dated June, without the year, which Mr Bain rightly, it seems, assigns to 1308. It sets out that the levies summoned to meet the king at Carlisle on 23 August shall be countermanded and that the king shall take no truce or sufferance from Bruce, but the Wardens of Scotland – Sir Robert de Umfraville, the Earl of Angus and Sir William de Ros of Hamelake (appointed on 21 June) – 'may take such, for as long time as possible, as they have done hitherto of their own power or by commission, so that the King, however, may furnish his castles with men and victuals, and that no one be taken or other "mesprision" made during such truce.' Then the wardens of districts are arranged. The Earl of Buchan, Sir John de Mowbray, and Sir Ingram de Um-fraville are to be Wardens of Galloway, Annandale and Car-rick respectively; Sir Alexander de Abernethy, Sir Edmund de Hastings and Sir John Fitz Marmaduke are to be wardens beyond the Forth. The endorsement bears that the Wardens of Scotland shall 'take truce from Robert de Brus as from themselves, as long as they can, but not beyond the month of Pasques' (April), and, curiously enough, that 'the King may break the truce at pleasure if the others will yield this point, but, if they will not, the truce may be made without it.' The memorandum testifies to the strength of Bruce's hold on the country and to the recalcitrance of Edward's barons. Still Edward struggled on. On 21 June, he requested a large number of officers to retain their posts until specified dates and to join the Scottish expedition at Carlisle on 23 August. On 10 July, he requisitioned ships and men from Shorehaul all round to Bristol, for the king 'needs a great fleet'. But on 11 August, he countermanded the order for these ships and men, 'the King having deferred his expedition for the present.' The English barons were too strong for the young king.

It is not clear at what date Bruce proceeded to reduce Argyll. Probably, however, he undertook the expedition immediately after the reduction of the north. If he conducted a six weeks' siege of Perth, and Sir William Oliphant was one of the defenders, he could not have been free to go west until the very end of July 1308. Fordun states that within a week after 15 August Bruce defeated the men of Argyll and subdued the whole land, that he then besieged Alexander of Argyll 'for some time' in Dunstaffnage Castle (some three miles from Oban) and that Alexander, on surrendering, refused to do homage but was allowed a safe-conduct for himself and his followers to England. Barbour tells how Lorn – John, the son of Alexander – gathered some 2000 men and opposed Bruce in a narrow pass between a steep mountain and the sheer bank of a loch – perhaps the Pass of Brander between Ben Cruachan and Loch Awe. Lorn held the loch in his boats and ambushed a party on the ridge commanding the pass. Bruce, having dispatched Douglas, Sir Alexander Fraser, Sir William Wiseman and Sir Andrew Gray with a body of archers to fetch a circuit above Lorn's ambush, boldly advanced up the pass. Lorn's men attacked, tumbling stones down the slope, but, finding themselves caught in the

85

rear, they fled downhill to a bridge crossing the river at one end of the loch and, having crossed, attempted to break down the bridge. Bruce was upon them before they could effect their purpose and completely defeated them. Having rapidly overrun Lorn's country, he took Dunstaffnage and received to his peace Alexander of Argyll, while John of Lorn, 'rebel as he was wont to be', escaped by water. Bruce then received the homage of all the men of Argyll and returned to Perth.

But these events must have been spread over a considerable time, and they may not have been continuous. The record of Bruce's parliament at St Andrews on 16 March 1309 places it beyond doubt that Alexander of Argyll came to Bruce's peace; it states that Alexander himself and 'the barons of the whole of Argyll and Inchegall' were present as liegemen of Bruce. Again, on 16 June 1309, both Alexander and John of Lorn were present at Edward's council at Westminster as liegemen of the English king. Further, we have a letter of Lorn's, undated but replying to a letter of Edward's dated 11 March, in which he says that he had been on his sickbed for half a year; that Bruce 'had approached his territories with 10,000 or 15,000 men, it was said, both by land and sea', while he 'had no more than 800 to oppose him' and 'the barons of Argyll gave him no aid'; that a truce had been made at the instance of Bruce; that 'he hears that Bruce, when he came, was boasting that he [Lorn] had come to his peace,' 'which God and he [Lorn] knows is not true'; that, on the contrary, 'he is, and will ever be, ready to serve him [Edward] to the utmost of his power'; that 'he has three castles to guard, and a loch twenty-four leagues long, on which he has vessels properly manned, but is not sure of his neighbours'; and that 'so soon as the King or his power arrives, he will be ready with lands, ships, and others to aid him,' either in person (if he is not sick) or by his son. Neglecting minor discrepancies, one may safely accept Mr Bain's reconciliation of the various accounts. Alexander came to Bruce's peace after the affair of Loch Awe; John was still holding out in March but was driven from Dunstaffnage within the next two months, and Alexander thereupon retired, with John, to England. Alexander died in Ireland at the end of 1310. John lived to fight for Edward some seven or eight years more, but, as Mr Bain gently remarks, 'Barbour has strangely misrepresented his later career.'

Bruce was now master in the west as well as in the north. Beyond Forth, however, Perth, if ever captured, must soon have been recovered; and Dundee – and even Banff – remained in English hands as well as the key fortress of Stirling on the south bank of the dividing river. Still Bruce was master of the country, and he was free to turn his attention to the south.

Sir Edward Bruce, after an arduous struggle, had taken a firm grip of Galloway by the end of 1308. With Lindsay, Boyd and Douglas he had attacked the Galwegians – 'notwithstanding the tribute they received from them,' says the Lanercost chronicler, who also admits that they 'subdued almost all that land.' According to Barbour, Sir Edward met the English near Cree, routed them, slew some 1200 and pursued Umfraville and St John to Buittle Castle. St John then rode to England and brought up over 1500 men. On hearing this, Sir Edward instantly mounted with 50 men, followed up the trail of the enemy in the morning mist and, when the day cleared and he found himself within bowshot, charged with his usual reckless audacity. The English believed there must be more men with Sir Edward than they saw. At the third charge he routed them, slaying or taking many, St John, however, escaping. Sir Allan de Cathcart, Barbour affirms, 'told me this tale.' Sir Edward had all Galloway at the king's peace.

Fordun, again, relates that Sir Edward, on 18 November, inflicted a crushing defeat on Donald of the Isles and the Galwegians on the River Dee (not Cree), taking Donald prisoner in his flight and slaying 'a knight named Roland, with many of the nobles of Galloway.' Whatever the dates and the details, Sir Edward must have done some stern fighting. The Lanercost chronicler even records that it was said that the English king would have liked, if he could, to give Bruce peace on terms of aiding him against his earls and barons.

No doubt the MacDowalls were uprooted. But Mr Bain seems somewhat lax in stating that 'before 1 April 1309, Sir Dougal, their head, had been driven into England, where for thirty years he and his family were obliged to remain to escape the vengeance of the Bruces.' On 1 April 1309, it is true, Sir Dougal received as a reward for his services, 'whereby he has become hated by the enemy', the manor of Temple Couton in Yorkshire, 'for the residence and support of his wife and children'. But he himself was constable of Dumfries Castle in 1311, sheriff also in 1312, and he had the mortification of surrendering the castle to Bruce on 7 February 1313. Edward made provision for him from time to time until his death (before 27 January 1328). A petition by his son and heir, Duncan, dated 1347, represents that Sir Dougal lost £100 in land for his allegiance to Edward I and Edward II, that Sir Dougal's brother was slain (in revenge for Bruce's two brothers), that the petitioner's eldest brother had been slain at Bannockburn and that he and his six

88

brothers were destitute. It shows a dark glimpse of the losing side.

In the meantime, according to Barbour, Douglas had done some useful work on his own account. Some time after Bruce went north, he went to Douglasdale again and placed an ambush near his ancestral castle. He sent fourteen men with sackfuls of grass on horses' backs to pass along as if bound for Lanark fair. Sir John Webton, the constable, sallied upon them, whereupon they cast down the sacks, threw off their frocks and, mounting their horses, showed fight. Douglas now broke ambush and cut off Webton from the castle, eventually slaying him and all his men. Barbour relates that there was found in Webton's pouch a letter from a lady engaging to marry him if he kept 'the auenturous castell of Douglas' for a year – a story worked up by Sir Walter Scott in his boldly unhistorical *Castle Dangerous*. Douglas took the castle and demolished it.

Douglas also, Barbour says, did a great deal of hard fighting in Selkirk Forest. On one occasion, in a house on the Water of Lyne (which joins the Tweed a few miles above Peebles), he lighted upon Sir Alexander Stewart of Bonkill, whose father, Sir John, distinguished himself so brilliantly at Falkirk, Randolph, Bruce's nephew, Sir Adam de Gordon and others who were really in search of himself. He surrounded the house and a fierce fight resulted. Gordon got away safely, but Douglas captured Stewart, who was wounded, and Randolph and took them next morning to the king – who, in that case, must already have returned south. Barbour tells of the proud bearing of Randolph and how Bruce put him 'in firm keeping' until he acknowledged his authority. This must have taken place before 4 March 1309, when Edward conferred on Sir Adam de Gordon

89

Randolph's forfeited manor of Stichill in Roxburghshire. Never afterwards did Randolph swerve from his uncle's allegiance.

Early in 1309 (14 January, Hemingburgh; 12 February, Lanercost chronicler), papal envoys came to Edward and Bruce at the instance of the French king and a truce was made, to run to 1 November. But Bruce is said to have ignored it in practice, and perhaps that is why a new sentence of excommunication was pronounced against him and his adherents in the summer of 1309.

On 18 June, Edward summoned his array, and on 30 July, he renewed the summons, requiring his army to muster at Newcastle at Michaelmas and declaring that the Scots had 'notoriously broken' the truce. Yet only three days later (2 August), he authorized the Earl of Ulster to treat with Bruce for peace, and on 21 August he renewed the commission and granted safe-conducts for Bruce's envoys, Sir Nigel Campbell and Sir John de Menteith, the captor of Wallace, who must have joined Bruce before 16 March when he was present at the St Andrews parliament. Still Edward hurried on his preparations. He had summoned auxiliaries from Wales (5 August) and filled afresh the chief offices in Scotland (16 August), and presently he appointed the Earl of Gloucester captain of the army of Scotland (14 September) and dispatched fresh wardens to the Marches (about 18 October).

Again, however, the pope intervened, and on 29 November, Edward granted full powers to four of his magnates to treat in his name for a truce. The wardens of the Marches, according to the Lanercost chronicler, had just forestalled the step by taking provisional truce until the middle of January, and Edward extended the period to 8 March and afterwards 'to summer' 1310 – for, says the chronicler, 'the English do not like to enter Scotland to war before summer, especially because of the lack of fodder for their horses.' Probably the extension to summer was arranged by the commission of seven appointed on 16 February headed by the Bishop of St Andrews.

There had been a full year of peace negotiations and futile truces with warlike preparation in the background. On 24 February 1310, Bruce's position was strengthened by a formal recognition of his royal title by a special meeting of the prelates and other clergy at Dundee. At the beginning of June 1310, there was an outbreak on the Border, the Priory of Coldstream being sacked and the prioress and nuns dispersed, and in the middle of the month the English fleet was ordered north to strengthen Perth and to harass the eastern seaboard. Then, on 15 August, Edward again mustered his army at Newcastle (Hemingburgh) or at Berwick (Lanercost chronicler). The Earls of Lancaster, Pembroke (Valence), Warwick and Hereford would not accompany him, displeased with his favour for Gaveston although professing to be absorbed in their duties as 'Ordainers', but they sent their feudal services. The Earls of Gloucester, Warenne and Cornwall (Gaveston) with Percy, Clifford and many other magnates did attend the muster. The expedition, according to Walsingham, was said to be a mere pretext to excuse the king from going to France to do fealty for his French possessions. He dreaded leaving Gaveston 'among his enemies' lest that troubler of the realm should 'meet death, prison, or worse'. 'Such things were said among the people, whether true or false,' says the chronicler, 'God knows, I don't.' The expedition crossed the Border early in September and passed by Selkirk, Roxburgh, Biggar, Lanark, Glasgow to Renfrew, back to Linlithgow

91

and from there to Berwick. The progress occupied just over two months. Bruce stood aloof; on 6 October, when Edward was at Biggar, he was reported to be with his forces 'on a moor near Stirling'. Fordun says there was famine in Scotland this year, many being reduced 'to feed on the flesh of horses and other unclean cattle'. But Edward was liberally supplied by the religious houses with 'oxen, cows, wethers, wheat, oats, barley, malt, beans, and peas' besides friendly contributions from other quarters. On 22 November, he issued a proclamation prohibiting the importation of provisions from England.

When Edward withdrew from Linlithgow, Bruce hung upon his rear through Lothian, severely harassing the army and all local sympathizers. Walsingham records an instance. A party of English and Welsh had gone out to plunder, supported by cavalry. Bruce suddenly attacked from ambush, and although aid quickly arrived, he killed 300 and retired as suddenly as he had advanced. 'Indeed,' says the chronicler, 'I should extol Bruce, whose policy was to fight thus and not in open field, but for his lying under the charge of homicide and the brand of treachery.'

Edward wintered at Berwick. Bruce seems to have actively developed offensive operations on the west coast to draw him home by a flank attack as well as to obtain supplies. For, on 15 and 16 December, Edward roused his officers in the northwestern counties and in Wales and Ireland to counteract Bruce's reported purpose 'to send his whole fleet in the present winter to take the Isle of Man, and seize all the supplies therein for the sustenance of his men'. Bruce's adherents in Man are stated to have caused much trouble and mischief. A week before Christmas, Clifford and Sir Robert Fitz Pain met Bruce at Selkirk to discuss terms of peace, and another interview was arranged with the Earls of Gloucester and Cornwall near Melrose; but 'it was said,' writes a high official on 19 February, 'that Bruce had been warned by some that he would be taken, and therefore departed, so that they have had no parley.'

A memorandum, undated but assignable to 1307–10, addressed by the 'Commune' of Scotland to Edward and his great officers in the country, affords a glimpse of the English high-handedness that always did so much to thwart the English policy. The Commons represent that 'though they have purchased a truce for the safety of the country and their allegiance, and included the castles and towns in their bounds – namely, the sheriffdoms of Berwick, Roxburgh, and Edinburgh,' yet 'some of the sheriffs allow no goods to leave their castles, or their garrisons to pay for what they buy' – the sheriff of Edinburgh, in particular – 'and the country is so poor that they cannot get on without ready money.' Again, 'when the enemy's people come to bargain under the truce, their goods are taken by some of the castellans and king's officers, endangering the truce, as the robbers are harboured in the castles.' They earnestly plead for redress of such oppressions and complain that the king's former letters on the subject have been suppressed by the officers to blame. Only an occupation in overwhelming force could stand against such a course of official misconduct. Meantime this fatal administrative weakness was greatly counterbalanced by the political divisions among the Scots.

In 1311, Gaveston, for whom Edward could find no resting place elsewhere, was established as lieutenant north of Forth and warden of Dundee and Perth. 'It is said,' writes an anonymous high official on 4 April 1311, 'that Bruce meant to fight with the Earl of Cornwall' (Gaveston), but either he

93

was unable to do so or deemed it prudent to weary out the enemy by harassing evasion. On 9 April, Edward issued instructions hastening the outfit of the fleet destined for the coast of Argyll under Sir John of that ilk – 'seeing it is one of the greatest movements of the Scottish war'; and throughout May and June great pressure was brought to bear upon the ports of England and Ireland, although not always with effect. On 14 July, the muster of the army at Roxburgh was postponed to 1 August. 'This expedition,' said Edward, 'lies especially close to our heart.'

Edward, however, was in deep trouble with his 'Ordainers', and Bruce forestalled him. On 12 August, he burst into England at the Solway, burned the whole of Gilsland, the town of Haltwhistle and a great part of Tyndale, returning to Scotland in eight days with great droves of cattle. The Lanercost chronicler admits that he killed few besides those who offered resistance and that, although he took several of the canons and did infinite mischief during the three days he made the monastery his headquarters, yet he released the canons of his own accord. The latter episode is recorded as a separate foray but probably it belongs to the August operations.

The same chronicler gives an account of a more serious raid on 8 September by way of Harbottle, Holystone and Redesdale, down to Corbridge and back through Tyndale, occupying fifteen days. The wardens of the Marches, he says, could offer no resistance and confined their efforts to wasting the country in anticipation of the Scots, only 'they did not burn houses or slay men'. The stress of opposition fell on the Bishop of Durham. Both Edward and the bishop paint the invasion in the usual lurid colours. At the same time the people had certainly not been handled with consideration. The Northumbrians protected themselves by payment of £2000 for a respite until 2 February 1312. In the middle of December Bruce appears to have made another raid into England, and on 26 January 1312, Edward appointed six commissioners to treat in his name for truce with the Scots.

The rising power of Bruce is variously testified otherwise than by the progress of his army. The Lanercost chronicler admits that, in spite of the adherence of so many Scots to the English side, 'their hearts, though not their persons, were always with their countrymen.'

An inquisition at Edinburgh on 20 February mentions seven landed knights and others who had gone over to Bruce in the past three or four years, including Sir Robert de Keith, Sir Thomas de la Haye and Sir Edmund de Ramsay. Again, a list of land rewards to Sir Robert de Hastang on 20 March mentions twelve, among whom are Sir David de Brechin (who, however, is made Warden of Berwick on 20 April although Sir Edmund de Hastings receives the post on 3 May), Sir Alexander de Lindsay, Sir Geoffrey de Mowbray and Sir Herbert de Maxwell. In five hard years Bruce had recovered three parts of his kingdom and carried fire and sword through the English March.

CHAPTER VIII

RECOVERY OF FORTRESSES

Bruce was now in a position to turn his main energies against the strongholds still in English occupation.

Towards the end of March 1312 he was preparing to besiege Berwick with an unusually large force. But the operations are not known and, in any case, they were soon postponed. On 26 April he held a parliament at Ayr and carefully settled the succession to the throne.

The dissensions between Edward and his barons appear to have induced Bruce to carry the war into the enemy's territory. While the incensed barons were hunting down Gaveston, he raided the March again, took tribute, burned Norham and carried off prisoners and booty. Again, at the end of June, after Gaveston was beheaded, Bruce made another foray into the episcopate of Durham. He burnt Hexham and dealt so severely with the Priory that even in 1320, it is said, the canons were unable to return, while their collectors were still 'wandering about in the country in 1326, with the archbishop's brief, in quest of funds for the canons and their church.' It may have been on this occasion that Bruce sent Douglas to pillage the region of Hartlepool. It is, no doubt, in reference to a subsequent raid, that the Lanercost chronicler tells how a detachment entered Durham on market day, burned most of the town and slew all who resisted but did not touch the castle or the abbey. For £2000 the episcopate bought peace until next midsummer, the Scots bargaining for free passage 'whenever they wanted to ride further into England!' The Palatinate Register records the date as 16 August. The Northumbrians, too, paid £2000. Westmorland, Coupland and Cumberland also paid ransom – money in part, and for the rest hostages, 'sons of the greater lords of the country'. And meantime Edward was squabbling with his barons. It was enough to make his martial father rise from his grave.

At last, on 6 December, the Lanercost chronicler relates, Bruce suddenly pounced on Berwick. His men had placed two ladders, and 'he would soon have had the castle, as is believed,' had the garrison not been warned by the barking of a dog. The ladders, says the chronicler, 'were of a remarkable make, as I myself, who write this, witnessed with my own eyes.' He describes ladders of ropes, with wooden steps and iron hooks to grip the wall top. The alarm being raised, Bruce retired, leaving the two ladders for the monk's inspection. 'So a dog on that occasion saved the town, as once geese by their cackling saved Rome.'

Bruce turned north to Perth. According to the Lanercost chronicler, he took the town by surprise on the night of 10 January (Fordun says 8 January) 1313. The governor, Sir William Oliphant – probably this is the capture of Perth antedated by Barbour – 'was bound and sent to the islands afar', but, if so, he did not stay long there, for he was in England within two months, and on 21 October he obtained a safe-conduct to return to Scotland. The chronicler says that Bruce slew the better Scots burgesses but permitted the English to go free, while Fordun records that he put 'the disloyal people, Scots and English alike', to the sword. 'In his clemency,' adds Fordun, 'he spared the rabble, and granted forgiveness to such as asked it; but he destroyed the walls and dykes, and consumed everything else with fire.'

Bruce next swept down upon Dumfries. Here his old enemy, Sir Dougal MacDowall, constable of the castle, had experienced much difficulty all through summer and autumn in obtaining adequate supplies. He gave up the castle to Bruce on 7 February, the short siege probably indicating that he was starved into surrender. It is likely, as Mr Bain surmises, that Buittle, Dalswinton, Lochmaben and Carlaverock were all recovered about the same time.

The Scots appear to have derived considerable supplies from Flanders. On 15 February 1313, Edward remonstrated with the Count of Flanders, begging him to restrain his subjects from all intercourse with Scotsmen.

The count seized the occasion to demand compensation for losses and injuries inflicted on his subjects by Englishmen. An English commission, much to the disgust of the Flemish envoys, rejected the claims, and presently Flemish seamen plundered English vessels, the chief depredator being the ingenious John Crab whom we shall meet again. On 1 May 1313, Edward invited the count to send his aggrieved subjects back to London but now, he added, 'we hear that thirteen ships of your power, laden with arms and victuals, quite lately crossed from the port of Swyn to Scotland – whereat we very much marvel.' The Flemish quarrel went on, but on 17 May, at the instance of the French king, Edward appointed four commissioners 'to negotiate a truce or sufferance with the Scots'.

Within a week, however, as Edward was on the point of embarking for France to confer with Philip about Gascony, he learned from a special messenger from the lieges of Cumberland that the Scots were again upon them. He could only tell them to do their best, and he would hasten back to take order for their safety. On 6 June, Bishop Kellawe of Durham testifies to the forlorn state of the nuns of Halistan on the March; there are hostile incursions daily, goods and cattle are reived (robbed), and the very nuns are insulted and persecuted by the robbers and driven from their homes suffering miserably. Such are examples of the state of affairs in the mind of the Lanercost chronicler when he records that 'the people of Northumberland, Westmorland, and Cumberland, and other men of the Marches, neither having nor hoping from their King defence or aid, he being then in the remote parts of England and not appearing to trouble himself about them, offered no moderate amount – nay a very large amount – of money to Robert for truce till 29 September 1314.' Bruce was striking hard and persistently, and Edward was giving way all along the line of war.

On his return, indeed, Edward at once took measures of retaliation. As early as 2 April he had answered applications from Northumberland for aid by a promise of relief before midsummer – a promise that remained unfulfilled. On 6 July he demanded a subsidy from the bishops, and on 13 August he made a similar appeal to the abbots and convents. In warlike mood at the end of July, he had ordered something like a pressgang muster of boats at the ports from the Wash round to Plymouth. It was only a spasmodic effort of weakness. About the beginning of October, Sir Ralph FitzWilliam reported that 'they are grievously menaced with treason at Berwick, but, if the garrison are loyal, they will defend it against the King of France and the King of Scotland for a while till succour reaches them.' At the end of the next month, the Bishop of St Andrews went to France in the interest of Edward, no doubt with the object of detaching Philip from cooperation with Bruce. It was a fatuous choice of envoy.

The wretched inefficiency of Edward had by this time rendered the position of his adherents in Scotland all but insupportable. In November they dispatched the Earl of March and Sir Adam de Gordon to lay their grievances before him. Their petition recounts their heavy losses at the hands of the enemy during the past three years, their costly purchase of truce and especially their intolerable sufferings from the lawless outrages committed upon them by the garrisons of Berwick and Roxburgh who are alleged to have plundered, killed and held them to ransom at will as if they had been enemies. Here is a substantial repetition of the memorandum of 1307–10. Sir Adam de Gordon could tell how he had himself been arrested by the constable of Roxburgh Castle and required to find security for his good behaviour. The king, replying on 28 November, could only give them the cold comfort of an assurance of his intention to march to their relief at next midsummer. It is quite natural that such slackness of the central authority should have encouraged such marauding scoundrels on the Border as Sir Gilbert de Middleton and Thomas de Pencaitland. That notorious knight of the road, Sir Gilbert, will cross our path again.

It could not have been earlier than autumn 1313 that Bruce recovered the Peel of Linlithgow which was held by Sir Archibald de Livingstone under the orders of Sir Peter Lubaud, warden and sheriff of Edinburgh. Barbour makes it harvest time. The peel garrison had cut their hay and engaged William Bunnock, a neighbouring farmer who hated them patriotically, to 'lead' it for them. Bunnock conceived the notion of elevating the familiar harvesting process to an operation of war and arranged the strategic details with his friends. He planted an ambush in the early morning and let the hay lie till the peel men had gone out to cut their crop. Loading the hay, with eight men hidden in it, he set a hardy yeoman with a hatchet under his belt to drive the waggon, himself walking idly beside it. When the waggon was half-way through the gate, Bunnock shouted the signal, 'Thief! Call all! Call all!' The driver instantly cut the traces, stopping the waggon; Bunnock slew the porter; the eight men leapt down from the midst of the hay, and the ambush swarmed up. They slew the men they found in the garrison and pursued those who were in the fields towards Edinburgh and Stirling, killing some in their flight. For this exploit Bruce rewarded Bunnock well. The peel he at once demolished. The story of Bunnock rests on the sole authority of Barbour.

The next castle to fall was Roxburgh. Douglas had been keeping the Forest and harassing Roxburgh and Jedburgh Castles. Resolving to win Roxburgh, he got a handy man, Simon of the Leadhouse, to make him ladders of hemp ropes with strong wooden steps and iron hooks after the Berwick pattern. Then gathering some sixty men, he approached the castle on Fastern's Even (Shrove Tuesday), 27 February 1314 and waited until dark. The party left their horses, put black frocks over their armour and crept forward on all fours like cattle. The deception succeeded. Barbour says they overheard the garrison jesting at the expense of the neighbouring farmer, who, they imagined, had left his cattle roaming free to be carried off by the Douglas. The click of a hook on the wall attracted a sentinel, but Simon, who had mounted first, stabbed the man dead, and the party quickly scaled the

101

wall. The garrison were making merry in the hall when the Scots burst in upon them with the Douglas war cry. A sharp conflict ensued. At length Sir William de Fiennes, the constable, a brave Gascon, retreated to the great tower.

With daylight, the Scots plied the tower with arrows and eventually wounded Sir William so badly in the face that he yielded on terms that he and his men should pass safe to England. Douglas conducted them over the Border, and Sir William soon afterwards died of his wound. Bruce sent his brother Sir Edward to demolish the castle. Sir Edward, says Barbour, secured all Teviotdale except Jedburgh and other places near the English border. On main points Barbour is corroborated by Sir Thomas Gray and the Lanercost chronicler.

The news of the capture of Roxburgh stimulated the rivalry of Randolph, who was besieging Sir Peter Lubaud in Edinburgh Castle. With no hope of taking the place by assault, Randolph cast about for some likely stratagem when William Francis (or William the Frenchman), one of his men, suggested a plan of extreme boldness. Francis, according to Barbour, stated that he had at one time lived in the castle and, having a sweetheart in the town, had been accustomed to climb the sheer rock on the darkest nights. All that was needed was good nerve and a twelve-foot ladder for the wall on the top. So, on a dark night – Fordun gives 14 March 1314 – Randolph with thirty picked men undertook the adventurous ascent. About halfway up they stopped to rest. Here their nerves were dramatically tested. One of the watch overhead threw down a stone, exclaiming 'Away! I see you well.' It was only a joke, the sentry saw nothing and the stone passed harmlessly over them. The watchmen passed on without suspicion, and Randolph with his men hastened up the steeper and steeper crag to the foot of the wall. Instantly the ladder was fixed, Francis mounting first, then Sir Andrew Gray and Randolph himself third. Before all the party got over, the watch was alarmed, the cry of 'Treason! Treason!' resounded through the castle, and a desperate struggle ensued. Randolph himself was sorely bested, but he succeeded in killing the commandant, whereupon the garrison gave in.

The Lanercost chronicler states that a strong assault was made on the south gate, the only point reasonably open to assault, where the garrison offered a vigorous resistance, and that the party mounting the rock on the north side under cover of this front attack, having surprised and overcome the defenders, opened the gate to their comrades. Sir Peter Lubaud, the warden, says Barbour, had been deposed from the command of the garrison on account of some suspicious intercourse with the enemy and was found by Randolph in prison in fetters. He became Bruce's man, but soon afterwards he fell under suspicion of treason and, by Bruce's order, was drawn and hanged (Gray), or at any rate put in prison, where he died miserably (John of Tynmouth). The Lanercost writer states that the victors 'slew the English', probably meaning the garrison, but the extant rolls show that there were many Scotsmen in the garrison, 'two of them,' as Mr Bain remarks, even 'bearing the surname of Douglas.' Bruce demolished the castle.

Barbour states that Sir Edward Bruce, having won all Galloway and Nithsdale and taken Rutherglen Peel and Dundee Castle, laid siege to Stirling Castle from Lent to midsummer 1313, and that then Sir Philip de Mowbray, the constable, agreed to yield the castle provided it were not relieved by midsummer 1314. The most recklessly chivalrous terms are indeed consonant with Sir Edward's character. But if, as Barbour and the Monk of Malmesbury agree, Mowbray was influenced by a threatened failure of provisions, the period must have been much less. He in Stirling would hardly be in any better case for supplies than was MacDowall in Dumfries. Immediately on the siege of the castle, he would begin to feel the pinch, and the fall of Edinburgh would at once intimate the hopelessness of his position. But, further, we have seen Sir Edward demolishing Roxburgh Castle in early March, and it does not seem likely that he would have left a substitute to look after Stirling. Besides, the Lanercost chronicler can hardly be mistaken when he says that Sir Edward entered England on 17 April, taking up his headquarters at the bishop's manor house at Rose and sending his army as far as Englewood Forest, south and west, for three days to burn and plunder because the tribute had not been duly paid. Once more, the Monk of Malmesbury represents that it was after the fall of the other castles that Mowbray carried to Edward the news of his agreement for surrender. On the whole, it may be seriously doubted whether the respite extended beyond a couple of months or even six weeks. It is not, apparently, until 27 May that Mowbray's conditional agreement for surrender is mentioned in any existing official document.

Besides Stirling, the only fortresses of any importance that now remained in the hands of the English were Berwick, Jedburgh and Bothwell. But the immediate interest centres on the fateful attempt to relieve the castle of Stirling.

CHAPTER IX

*T*HE BATTLE OF
BANNOCKBURN

As far back as 23 December Edward II had summoned his
army to assemble at Berwick on 10 June 1314 for the war
against Scotland. In March, he was busily ordering his fleet
for service on the east and west coasts and hastening the
muster of the Irish contingent under the Lord of Ulster. On
27 May, from New Abbey, he issued an urgent reminder to
the sheriffs and barons of the northern and midland counties
to have their men at Wark by 10 June. He has learnt, he tells
them, that the Scots are massing great numbers of foot in
strong positions protected by marshes and all but inaccessible
to cavalry; and he fires their zeal by informing them of the
agreement of Mowbray to surrender the castle of Stirling
unless the siege is raised by midsummer day. Bruce, then,
had already chosen his ground and started on his measures of
defence.

The English and Welsh troops summoned on 27 May
numbered together 21,540. The numbers of the Irish contingent are not preserved, but on analogous cases they can
hardly be reckoned beyond 3000. The Gascons, Hainaulters
and other foreigners are not likely to have numbered more
than the Irish. 'After allowing,' with Mr Bain, '10,000 light
horsemen and 3000 heavy cavalry, the whole English army

probably did not exceed 50,000' at the very outside. The Earls of Lancaster, Warenne, Arundel and Warwick did not join the expedition on the ostensible ground that the king had not first consulted parliament in conformity with the Ordinances and thus they would be laid open to ecclesiastical censure, but they sent their feudal services. The outfit of the army was on the most ample, not to say magnificent, scale. 'The multitude of waggons, if extended one after another in file,' says the Monk of Malmesbury, 'would have stretched over twenty leagues.' In truth, he says, it was universally acknowledged that 'such an army did not go out of England in our time.' The Monk's testimony lends a sober colour to the assertion of Robert Baston, the Carmelite friar who went to celebrate an English victory and was captured and made to sing the Scottish triumph. 'Never,' he declared, 'was seen a more splendid, noble, or proud English army.'

There is no definite clue to the numbers of the Scots. 'But,' as Mr Bain says, 'in so poor and thinly populated a country, devastated by long war, 15,000 or 16,000 would be a fair estimate of the comrades of Bruce. The Scots, twenty years later, could raise no more for the almost equally important object of relieving Berwick.'

The estimates usually given follow Barbour who says there were over 100,000 English – enough 'to conquer the whole world' – and some 50,000 Scots, of whom 30,000 were fighting men. No doubt Barbour includes in the English 100,000 the miscellaneous 'pitaille' or hangers-on who swarmed about the baggage trains of mediaeval armies. But Mr Bain's estimate seems to be as near as the authorities will admit. The proportion of English to Scots was most probably somewhere about three to one.

The army that mustered under Edward was indeed 'very

fair and great', yet, in the eyes of the Church, probably en-
lightened by later events, there was one needful thing lacking. When Edward I was on the warpath towards Scotland,
says the Lanercost chronicler, 'he was wont to visit on his
way the saints of England – Thomas of Canterbury, Edmund, Hugh, William, Cuthbert – and to offer them fair
oblations, to commend himself to their prayers, and to dis-
pense large gifts to the monasteries and the poor'; but his
degenerate son, omitting these pious duties, 'came with
great pomp and circumstance, took the goods of the monasteries on his route, and, it was stated, did and said some
things to the prejudice and injury of the saints,' by reason
whereof 'certain religious of England prophesied' that no good
would come of the expedition. To the same effect, Robert
of Reading records that Edward permitted his troops on
their march to ravage with violence the patrimony of 'religious' and other churchmen, as if they had been robbers
(*more praedonum*). Still the Archbishop of York and the
Bishop of Durham, rehearsing the long list of Bruce's alleged enormities, officially enjoined all within their juris-
diction to pray for the success of the king's arms, offering an
indulgence of forty days in reward of such patriotic piety.

The king was in high spirits over the splendour of his
army. Apparently he anticipated an easy and complete triumph. He started from Berwick only a few days before the
fateful day of St John. 'From day to day,' says the Monk of
Malmesbury, 'he hastened to the place fixed on beforehand,
not like a man leading an army to battle, but rather as if he
were going on pilgrimage to Compostella. Short was the
stay for sleep; shorter still the stay for food; in consequence
of which the horses, horsemen, and foot were worn out by
labour and fatigue.' On Friday 21 June the English army lay

at Edinburgh and on Saturday it lay at Falkirk, little more than ten miles from Stirling.

The problem for Bruce was to keep the English out of Stirling until St John's Day had passed. In good time he had selected and laid out the inevitable field of battle with military prescience of the first order. He had mustered his forces in the Torwood, in a position commanding the approach to Stirling from the south, and on the morning of Saturday 22 June, on news of the approach of the English, he marched them to the chosen spot on a plain some two miles south of Stirling within the last large loop of the Bannock Burn, called the New Park – a hunting ground of the Scots kings. The Park was a piece of firm ground rising on the north and west into the swelling ridges of Coxet Hill near St Ninian's and Gillies Hill on the left of the Bannock above the bend towards the Forth. Eastwards it fell away into a marshy tract filling the angle of the two rivers and intersected by watercourses. Southwards too, the hard ground was broken by two morasses – Halbert's Bog and Milton Bog – between the Park and the Bannock. Bruce rested his right wing on the steep bank of the Bannock below Gillies Hill; his left wing stretched away past St Ninian's nearly to the gates of Stirling; his rear was protected by Gillies Hill and the Bannock behind.

The English would be compelled to advance either across the Bannock between Parkmill and Beaton's Mill – a breadth of a short mile, free from precipitous banks – to the line of hard ground with a contracted front to be immediately divided by the intervening bogs, or else along the line of low and marshy flat between the Park and the Forth. To reduce the superiority of the English cavalry, Bruce had industriously dug pits along the parts of the firm route by

108

which they would probably, if not inevitably, advance – pits a foot wide, round and as deep as a man's knee, honeycombing the ground. These holes he covered loosely with a disguise of brushwood, turf and grass. He is also said to have inserted in them stakes shod with iron points. Sir Thomas de la Moore mentions long transverse trenches similarly covered so as to bear men aware of them but not horses. Later writers add that Bruce strewed the ground with calthrops, or metal spikes, to cripple the English horses. He himself had determined to fight on foot.

Bruce marshalled his troops in four divisions facing southeastwards. The van was led by Randolph. The second and third divisions were ranged behind the wings of the van, the former to the right and resting on the Bannock led by Sir Edward Bruce, the latter by Walter the Steward ('that then was but a beardless hyne') and Douglas. The rearguard, consisting of the men of Carrick, Argyll, Kintyre and the Isles, was stationed right behind the van at some interval, under the immediate command of Bruce himself. All the divisions could thus be promptly massed on the English whether they should select the higher or the lower line of advance. It was of the first importance that no detachment of the English should be allowed to outmanoeuvre the main body of the Scots and throw themselves into Stirling. Randolph, who held the most advanced position, was especially charged to guard against this fatal contingency. The noncombatants retired behind the hill in the rear, afterwards named from them the Gillies' (that is 'Servants') Hill.

The dispositions of the English army are not known in certain detail. There is little help in Barbour's statement that it was divided into ten companies of 10,000 each.

We know that the van was led by the Earl of Gloucester

109

and that, if Robert of Reading and the Monk of Malmesbury may be relied on, the appointment of Gloucester was hotly resented by the hereditary constable, the Earl of Hereford. The king's bridle was attended by Sir Aymer de Valence and Sir Giles d'Argentine, the latter of whom was rewarded as the third knight in Christendom and had been released from captivity in Salonica at the end of the preceding year through Edward's urgent representations to the emperor, and even to the empress, of Constantinople.

At sunrise on Sunday 23 June, the eve of St John, the Scots heard mass. Bruce then devoted special attention to the pits that were still being prepared. After midday – the Scots observed the fast on bread and water – the English were reported to be advancing from the fringe of the Torwood. Bruce issued his final orders. Then he is said to have addressed his men in terms of high resolution, bidding every man depart who was not ready for either alternative – to conquer or to die. Not a man moved from the ranks. More than five centuries later, at Balaclava, 'Men,' cried Sir Colin Campbell, 'you must die where you stand.' 'Ay, ay, Sir Colin, we'll do that,' was the cheery response. Such too was the spirit of the same race on the field of Bannockburn.

At this point, according to Barbour, Douglas and Sir Robert de Keith (hereditary marshal) proceeded, by order of Bruce, to reconnoitre the enemy's advance. They returned with such a report of the numbers and equipment of the English as they deemed it prudent to render to Bruce only 'in great privity'. Bruce, however, put a bold face on the situation and directed them, says Barbour, to spread a depreciatory account of the enemy.

The main body of the English appears to have halted while the leaders took counsel. But Gloucester, with the vanguard, ignorant of this and ardent for the fray, dashed through the Bannock and advanced on the Park where Sir Edward Bruce was ready to receive him. King Robert himself was riding in front of Sir Edward's division on a small palfrey with only a battle-axe in hand. On his basnet, according to Barbour's haberdashery, he wore a hat of jacked leather surmounted by 'a high crown, in token that he was a king'. Some of the English knights, says the Monk of Malmesbury, rode out between the lines and flung their challenges to the Scots. Sir Henry de Bohun, a knight of the house of Hereford, spurred at Bruce himself, and Bruce, swerving at the critical moment of attack, rose in his stirrups as de Bohun passed and split his head at a stroke, the shaft of his axe shivering in his hand. It may be remarked incidentally that Gray calls the luckless knight Sir Piers de Mountforth. The Scots pressed forward, the English fell back, but Bruce prudently soon recalled his men from the conflict. The Monk of Malmesbury, however, acknowledges that there was 'sufficiently keen fighting, in which Gloucester was unhorsed'. It is not surprising that the leading Scots remonstrated earnestly with Bruce for exposing himself to such an unequal chance. According to Barbour, he made no answer, only regretting the breaking of his good axe shaft. There can hardly be any doubt that Bruce took the risk deliberately, in calculated reliance on his dexterity and strength and not without a judicious eye to the moral effect on both armies. The feat, in any case, damped the ardour of the English and raised the spirit of the Scots.

Almost contemporaneously with the advance of Gloucester, Clifford and Beaumont, with 300 men-at-arms – Gray, whose father rode with them, says 300, while Barbour makes them 800 – hurried along the lower ground on the

English right towards Stirling. Their evident object, as Barbour says, was to relieve the castle, but the Lanercost chronicler ingenuously explains that it was to prevent the Scots from escaping by flight. Randolph, strangely ill-served by his scouts and by his eyes, if Barbour is right, is said not to have been aware of the movement until he received a sharp message from Bruce (as if Bruce's attention was not fully engaged elsewhere), telling him significantly that a rose had fallen from his chaplet. This is sheer monkish imagination. Gray makes no mention of this incredible inadvertence but represents Randolph as fired by the news of Bruce's repulse of the English van, and the Lanercost chronicler states that the Scots deliberately allowed the advance of the party. Of course they did – Randolph undoubtedly saw them the moment they moved onto the carse. To do so was no less important than it was for Sir Edward to be ready for Gloucester's onset. The next step for Randolph was to tackle his enemy at the right spot and not elsewhere. With a strong detachment he rapidly traversed the wooded edge of the Park so as to converge upon the English horsemen at the narrow neck between St Ninian's and the Forth – the only point, in fact, where he could calculate upon holding them without moving his whole division down into the low-lying ground (if even that would have done it) and deranging the order of battle. When they were 'neath the kirk, he issued from the wood and menaced their further progress.

'Let us retire a little,' said Beaumont; 'let them come; give them the fields.'

'Sir,' remarked Sir Thomas Gray, the elder, 'I suspect if you give them so much now, they will have all only too soon.'

'Why,' rejoined Beaumont tartly, 'if you are afraid you can flee.'

'Sir,' replied Gray, 'it is not for fear that I shall flee this day.'

Whereupon Sir Thomas spurred his horse between Beaumont and Sir William d'Eyncourt and charged the Scots. Randolph, whose men were on foot, instantly threw them into a schiltron, 'like a hedgehog'. D'Eyncourt was slain at the first onset. Gray's horse was speared and he himself was taken prisoner. The horsemen were wholly unable to make the slightest impression on the schiltron: they could not ride down the Scots; they could only cast spears and other missiles into their midst. Occasionally, on the other hand, a Scot would leap out from the ranks and strike down horse or rider. Douglas, seeing the Scots surrounded, entreated Bruce to permit him to go to Randolph's aid. Bruce, however, sternly refused to disorder his array but at last yielded to his urging. The temporary absence of Douglas and a small party could not really matter at the moment, and it was wise to make doubly sure of the vital object dependent on Randolph's defence. On getting near, however, and perceiving that Randolph was holding his own, Douglas chivalrously halted his men. But his appearance was not without effect upon the English party. They gave up the contest. The movement had completely failed. Some of them straggled to Stirling Castle, the main body of the survivors fled back the way they had come, and Randolph returned in triumph. It may be, as Barbour says, that Bruce used the occasion to deliver to his men another rousing address. At any rate he had gained a marked success in each of the operations of the day.

Although Gloucester had retired, apparently he did not withdraw beyond the Bannock but encamped for the night along the north bank. According to the unanimous testimony of the chroniclers, the English host was struck with serious discouragement. It may have been, as Barbour says, that they talked in groups disconsolately and forebodingly, and that the encouragement of the leaders predicting victory in the great battle on the morrow failed to shake off their depression. Still there was activity in the vanguard camp. Barbour says that at night efforts were made to render bad parts of the low-lying land in the angle of the rivers passable and even that help in this work was provided by the Stirling garrison. According to the Malmesbury chronicler, the English anticipated attack in the night, and Gray states that they lay under arms, their horses being ready bridled. Bruce, however, had resolutely restricted himself to the tactics of defence, but the anticipation was natural enough. Some of the men, very probably, sought artificial means of consolation and courage. Sir Thomas de la Moore, following Baston, pictures the English camp as a lamentable and unwonted scene of drunkenness, men 'shouting "Wassail" and "Drinkhail" beyond ordinary', and he sets forth in forcible contrast the quiet self-restraint and patriotic confidence of the Scots

In all the circumstances, it would seem an inexplicable thing that the Scots should have been on the point of retiring in the night and making for the fastnesses of the Lennox. Yet Gray records that such was their intention. Sir Alexander de Seton, he says, came secretly from the English army to Bruce and told him that they had lost heart and would certainly give way before a vigorous onset next day, whereupon Bruce changed his plans and braced himself to fight on the morrow. The Scots had, indeed, 'done enough for the day', but they had not done enough for the occasion. Stirling Castle might yet be relieved. It is likely enough that Seton visited Bruce and that there were weak-kneed warriors in Bruce's lines, but that the matter of the interview is correctly reported by Gray seems absolutely incredible.

On the morning of St John's Day, 24 June, the Scots heard mass at sunrise, broke their fast and lined up with all banners displayed. Bruce made some new knights and created Walter the Steward and Douglas bannerets. He then made fresh dispositions of his troops in view of the position of the English van along the Bannock. There, clearly, the battle would be fought. Accordingly, he brought forward Randolph's division from the wood, placing it probably by the northwest corner of Halbert's Bog, almost parallel to Sir Edward's division, while the third division lay across the southeast slopes of Coxet Hill. The formation was in echelon by the right with unequal intervals. Behind the general line, the rear division stretched from the southwest slopes of Coxet Hill towards Gillies Hill.

The Scottish array appears to have made a deeper impression on the English veterans than on the English king. The Malmesbury chronicler states that the more experienced leaders advised that the battle should be postponed until the following day, partly because of the solemn feast, partly because of the fatigue of the soldiery. The advice was scorned by the younger knights. It was supported, however, by Gloucester, himself a youthful knight. On him, it is said, the king turned with vehement indignation, charging him even with treason and double-dealing. 'Today,' replied the Earl, 'it will be clear that I am neither traitor nor double-dealer', and he addressed himself to preparation for battle.

The Scots seem to have made a paltry show in the eyes of Edward. 'What! Will yonder Scots fight?' he is said to have asked his attendant knights incredulously. Sir Ingram de Umfraville assured him they would, at the same time suggesting that the English should pretend to retire and so draw the Scots from their ranks to plunder when they would fall

115

easy victims. Neither did this suggestion fit with the high humour of Edward. At the moment, he observed the Scottish ranks falling on their knees as the Abbot of Inchaffray passed along the lines bearing aloft the crucifix.

'Yon folk kneel to ask for mercy,' he exclaimed.

'Sire,' said Umfraville, 'ye say sooth now; they crave mercy, but not of you; it is to God they cry for their trespasses. I tell you of a surety, yonder men will win or die'.

'So be it!' cried Edward, 'we shall soon see.' And he ordered the trumpets to sound the charge.

At the very moment when the hostile armies were closing in stern conflict, says the Monk of Malmesbury, Gloucester and Hereford were wrangling over the question of precedence, and Gloucester sprang forward, 'inordinately bent on carrying off a triumph at the first onset'. His heavy cavalry, although hampered for space and disconcerted by the treacherous pits, went forward gallantly under the cover of a strong force of archers who severely galled the Scots and even drove back their bowmen. They crashed against Sir Edward Bruce's division, which received them 'like a dense hedge' or 'wood'. The great horses with their eager riders dashed themselves in vain against the solid and impenetrable schiltron. Those behind pressed forward, only to bite the dust, like their comrades, under the spears and axes of the Scots. 'There,' says the Monk of Malmesbury, 'the horrible crash of splintered spears, the terrible clangour of swords quivering on helmets, the insupportable force of the Scottish axes, the fearsome cloud of arrows and darts discharged on both sides, might have shaken the courage of the very stoutest heart. The redoubling of blow on blow, the vociferation of encouragements, the din of universal shouting, and the groans of the dying could be heard farther than may

116

be said.' The Lanercost writer goes near to justifying Scott's remarkable expression, 'steeds that shriek in agony'. Seldom in history has there been so fierce a turmoil of battle.

According to Barbour, Randolph, noting the strain on the first division, bore down to Sir Edward's support and drew an equally heavy attack upon himself. Steadily the second division won ground, although they seemed lost in the swarms of the enemy 'as they were plunged in the sea'. But not yet did victory incline to either side. Then Bruce threw into the scale the weight of the third division, the Steward and Douglas ranging themselves 'beside the Earl a little by'. With splendid tenacity, the English grappled with the new-comers in stubborn conflict until, Barbour says, 'the blood stood in pools' on the field.

The engagement was now as general as the nature of the position allowed. Both sides settled down to steady hard pounding, and it remained to be seen which would pound the hardest and the longest.

The English were at an enormous disadvantage in being unable to bring into action their whole force together. They could, indeed, supply the gaps in the narrow front with sheer weight of pressure from the rear, and they took bold risks on parts of the softer ground, especially along the north bank of the Bannock, but even so the fighting line was grievously hampered for space and the wild career of wounded horses defied the most strenuous efforts to pre-serve order. The archers, however, worked round to the right of Sir Edward's division, plying their bows with such energy and discrimination as greatly to disconcert Sir Edward's men. The moment had come for King Robert to or-der into action the marshal, Sir Robert de Keith, with his handful of 500 horsemen 'armed in steel'. Keith dashed upon the archers in flank and scattered them in flight. This successful operation gave the Scots archers the opportunity to retaliate with effect while it relieved the foremost division to reconcentrate their energies on the heavy cavalry steadily thundering on their front. But more English cavalry pressed to occupy the ground abandoned by the English archers. And now Bruce appears to have brought his rear division into action upon the English flank. It was his last resource. The Scots, says Barbour, 'fought as they were in a rage; they laid on as men out of wit.' But still the English disputed every inch of ground with indomitable resolution.

It was probably about this time that the gallant young Gloucester fell. After brilliant efforts to penetrate the impenetrable wedge of Scots, he had his horse slain under him and was thrown to the ground. The mishap is said to have dazed his men, who 'stood as if astonied' instead of aiding him to rise, burdened as he was with the weight of his armour and possibly trampled by his horse. He was thus slain in the midst of the 500 armed followers he had led into the front of the battle. The Monk of Malmesbury raises a loud lament over Gloucester's luckless fate: 'Devil take soldiery,' he exclaims in pious energy, 'whose courage oozes out at the critical moment of need.' It may be, however, that others are right in stating that Gloucester was slain in consequence of his rash and headlong advance at the very first onset.

The prolonged and doubtful struggle naturally wearied out the patience of the noncombatants behind Gillies Hill. Choosing a captain, says Barbour, they marshalled themselves – 15,000 to 20,000 in number – improvised banners by fastening sheets on boughs and spears and advanced over the brow of the hill in view of the battle raging below. The English, it is said, believing them to be a fresh army, were struck with panic. Bruce marking the effect shouted his war cry and urged his men to their utmost efforts. The English van at last yielded ground, although not at all points. The Scots, however, seized their advantage and pressed with all their might. The English line broke, falling back on the Bannock. Confusion increased at every step. Horsemen and foot, gentle and simple, were driven pell-mell into the Bannock and only a few were lucky enough to gain the south bank. The burn, Barbour says, was 'so full of horses and men that one might pass over it dry-shod.' The panic ran through the whole English army. The day was lost and won.

King Edward refused to believe the evidence of his senses and obstinately refused to quit the field. But it is the merest bravado – although countenanced by Scott – when Trokelowe relates how the king, in the bitterness and fury of his wrath, 'rushed truculently upon the enemy like a lion robbed of whelps', copiously shed their blood and was with difficulty withdrawn from the orgy of massacre. Unquestionably he stood aloof from the battle, watching its progress at a safe distance. When the English gave way in hopeless rout, Valence and Argentine seized his rein and hurried him off the field in spite of all remonstrance. It was not a moment too soon, for already, says Gray, Scots knights 'hung with their hands on the trappings of the King's destrier' (warhorse) in a determined attempt to capture him and were disengaged only by the king's desperate wielding of a mace. They had even ripped up his destrier so that presently he had to mount another. Once the king was clear of immediate pursuers, Argentine directed him to Stirling Castle and bade him farewell. 'I have not hitherto been accustomed to flee,' he said, 'nor will I flee now. I commend you to God.' And striking spurs to his steed he charged furiously upon Sir

119

Edward Bruce's division, but was quickly borne down and slain.

The turning of the king's rein was the signal for the general dispersal of the army in flight.

King Edward, attended by Valence, Despenser, Beaumont, Sir John de Cromwell and some 500 men-at-arms, made for Stirling Castle. Mowbray, with the plainest common sense – the suggestion of treachery is preposterous – begged him not to stay, for the castle must be surrendered; in any case, it would be taken. So the king was conducted in all haste round the Park and the Torwood towards Linlithgow. The Lanercost writer assigns as guide 'a certain Scots knight, who knew by what ways they could escape'. But for Bruce's anxious care to keep his men in hand in case of a rally, it seems quite certain that Edward would not have escaped at all. Douglas went in pursuit, but he had only some sixty horsemen. On the borders of the Torwood he met Sir Lawrence de Abernethy, who was coming to assist the English but at once changed sides on learning the issue of the day and joined Douglas in pursuit of the fugitive king. At Linlithgow Douglas came within bowshot of the royal party but not being strong enough to attack hung close upon their rear, capturing or killing the stragglers. The pursuit was continued hot-foot through Lothian; Douglas

> 'was alwais by thame neir;
> He leit thame nocht haf sic laseir
> As anys wattir for to ma' –

until at last Edward found shelter in Earl Patrick's castle of Dunbar. The king, with seventeen of his closest attendants, presently embarked on a vessel for Berwick (Barbour says

120

Bamborough), 'abandoning all the others,' sneers the Lanercost writer, 'to their fortune.' These others, according to Barbour, had not even been admitted to Dunbar Castle, but Douglas let them go on to Berwick unmolested and with a drove of captured horses speedily rejoined Bruce at Stirling. Sir Thomas de la Moore attributes the king's escape 'not to the swiftness of his horse, nor to the efforts of men, but to the Mother of God, whom he invoked', vowing to build and dedicate to her a house for twenty-four poor Carmelites, students of theology. This vow he fulfilled in spite of the dissuasion of Despenser, his favourite, and the house is now Oriel College, Oxford.

Another party, headed by the Earl of Hereford, made for Carlisle. According to the Lanercost chronicler, it included the Earl of Angus, Sir John de Segrave, Sir Antony de Lucy, Sir Ingram de Umfraville and many other knights, and numbered 600 horse and 1000 foot. They appealed to the hospitality of Sir Walter FitzGilbert, who held Valence's castle of Bothwell for Edward with a garrison of sixty Scots. FitzGilbert admitted 'the more noble' of them – Barbour says fifty, the Meaux chronicler, 120; Walsingham, a still larger number. FitzGilbert at once secured them all as prisoners and delivered them to Sir Edward Bruce who was sent with a large force to take them over. Hereford and others were eventually exchanged for the queen, Princess Marjory and the Bishop of Glasgow; the rest were held to heavy ransom. The main body of the party struggled forward to the Border, but many of them – Barbour says three-fourths – were slain or captured. Everywhere, in fact, the inhabitants, who 'had previously feigned peace' with the English, rose upon the hapless fugitives. Thus, Sir Maurice de Berkeley escaped with a great body of Welshmen, but, says Barbour,

121

many were taken or slain before they reached England. A large number fled to Stirling Castle where Barbour pictures the crags as covered with them, but these at once surrendered to a detachment of Bruce's force

It is hopeless to number the slain that strewed the field of battle, choked the Bannock or floated down the Forth. Barbour says roundly that 30,000 English were slain or drowned. The Meaux chronicler admits 20,000. Walsingham numbers no fewer than 700 knights and squires. Besides Gloucester and Argentine, the veteran Sir Robert de Clifford, Sir Pagan de Tybetot, Sir William the Marshal, Sir William de Vescy, Sir John Comyn (the son of the Red Comyn, slain at Dumfries), Sir Henry de Bohun, Sir William D'Eyncourt and many other notable warriors had fallen in the forefront of battle. Sir Edmund de Mauley, the king's steward, was drowned in the Bannock. The undistinguished many must remain uncounted. The Scots losses which, although comparatively insignificant, must still have been considerable, are equally beyond reckoning. The only men of note mentioned are Sir William Vipont and Sir Walter Ross.

In dealing with his prisoners, Bruce displayed a princely generosity. Trokelowe frankly acknowledges that his handsome liberality gained him immense respect 'even among his enemies'. Walsingham declares that it 'changed the hearts of many to love of him'. The Monk of Reading is fairly astonished. There was no haggling over exchanges or ransoms, although no doubt many of the ransoms were of a high figure. Sir Ralph de Monthermer, who was captured at Stirling and was an old friend of Bruce's, was released without ransom and carried back to England the king's shield, which Bruce freely returned. Sir Marmaduke Twenge, a relative of Bruce, who yielded himself to the king personally on the day after the battle, was sent home not only without ransom but with handsome gifts. The bodies of Gloucester and Clifford were freely sent to Edward at Berwick with every token of respect for gallant foes, and while the common men who fell on the field were interred in common trenches, the more noble were buried with noble ceremonial 'in holy places'.

The spoils collected by the victors were enormous. Walsingham ventures on an estimate of £200,000; 'so many good nobles, vigorous youths, noble horses, warlike arms, precious garments and napery, and vessels of gold – all lost!' Bruce made generous distribution among his valiant men. The individual ransoms largely increased the individual acquisitions. 'The whole land,' says Fordun, 'overflowed with boundless wealth.'

The chroniclers labour to assign reasons for the great disaster. The religious reason seems rather thin; for, if Edward and his barons broke the Ordinances and also fought on a feast day, Bruce and his friends lay under multiplied excommunications. There is more substance in other allegations – presumptuous confidence on the part of the English leaders, discord in their councils, their impetuous and disorderly advance, the fatigue and hunger of the men as a result of the rapid march from Berwick. One would be unwilling to press a certain lack of enthusiasm for their king or a suspicion of inadequate generalship. There is sufficient explanation in the skill, prudence and iron resolution of Bruce, supported by able generals of division and by brave and patriotic men. Had the result been otherwise, it would have been, for England, a greater disaster still.

'Yet' – and the word of honest sympathy and justification will not jar now on any generous mind:

'Yet mourn not, Land of Fame!
Though ne'er the leopards on thy shield
Retreated from so sad a field
Since Norman William came.
Oft may thine annals justly boast
Of battles stern by Scotland lost;
Grudge not her victory
When for her freeborn rights she strove –
Rights dear to all who Freedom love,
To none so dear as thee!'

CHAPTER X

INVASION OF ENGLAND AND IRELAND

The battle of Bannockburn might well have been the historical as well as the dramatic close of the struggle. But Edward refused to be taught by experience, and the desultory welter of war was miserably prolonged for nearly half a generation to come. The disaster rankled in Edward's mind, ever craving vengeance impotently. With childish wilfulness, he would not even concede to Bruce the formal title of King of Scots, although the Lanercost chronicler admits that the victory at Bannockburn extorted a general recognition of his right by conquest.

Edward retired from Berwick to York. It was plain that Bruce would instantly follow up his victory and already there was anxiety on the Border. Berwick was not only worried by the Scots but still more seriously menaced by the violence of the Northumbrians who had been angered by the hanging of a number of their countrymen for alleged treachery. The storm burst upon the north of England before Edward could send up reinforcements. Before the middle of July, Sir Andrew de Harcla, the constable of Carlisle, was daily expecting an attack and complained that he was hampered by lack of promised support. Bishop Kellawe could not attend parliament, so busy was he in preparations for the defence of his episcopate – 'all the people say that, if he now leave the district, they will not venture to stay behind.'

Immediately after the battle, Sir Philip de Mowbray surrendered Stirling Castle and passed over to the side of the victor. Towards the end of July, Sir Edward Bruce and Douglas, with other Scots nobles, crossed the eastern Border and ravaged Northumberland, leaving the castles unassailed. They spared the episcopate of Durham from fire in consideration of a large sum of money. Crossing the Tees, they penetrated beyond Richmond, the people fleeing before them to the south, to the woods, to the castles. They turned up Swaledale and on Stainmoor severely handled Harcla who had seized the opportunity of quietness at Carlisle to make a luckless raid upon them. On their northward march they burnt Brough, Appleby, Kirkoswald and other towns and trampled down the crops remorselessly. Coupland bought off a visitation. They re-entered Scotland with many prisoners for ransom and with great droves of cattle. They had met with no resistance except Harcla's futile effort. 'The English,' says Walsingham dolefully, 'had lost so much of their accustomed boldness that a hundred of them fled from the face of two or three Scots.'

On 9 September Edward held a parliament at York. He readily confirmed the ordinances, changed ministers, even retired Despenser – anything for the military help of his barons. But further operations against Scotland were postponed until Hereford and the other prisoners of note could be ransomed home. About a week later, Edward had a communication from Bruce expressing a strong desire for accord and amity. Safe-conducts were issued and truce commissioners were appointed. Meantime, however, the negotiations were too slow for the Scots, for on the very day that Edward appointed his commissioners, the Prior and Convent of Durham signed a bond for 800 marks to Randolph for a quiet life until the middle of January. Randolph, in fact, penetrated Yorkshire, committing the usual depredations. Still the negotiations, which apparently had been entered into at the instance of Philip of France, went forward. But in November the English envoys returned from Dumfries with empty hands and with the news of the likelihood of another invasion by the Scots, 'owing to the lack of food in their country'. Already, indeed, a body of Scots had occupied Tyndale and were pushing down towards Newcastle. About Christmas they again ravaged Northumberland and let off Cumberland until midsummer day the next year for the sum of 600 marks. The Archbishop of York, whose manor of Hexham had suffered, vigorously denounced the invaders, and at York Minster on 17 January barons and clergy resolved on making a stand at Northallerton three days later. But the only serious effort of the season was Harcla's November raid on Dumfriesshire where he was well punished despite the local knowledge of his disloyal lieutenant, Sir Thomas de Torthorwald. About the beginning of February, indeed, John of Argyll overpowered the Scots in the Isle of Man and recovered it for Edward, but 'the terror that prevailed throughout the north of England,' as Canon Raine says, 'was something unexampled,' 'with the exception of a few fortresses, two or three of the northern counties were almost permanently occupied by the Scots.'

On 26 April 1315, a parliament was held in the parish church of Ayr to consider 'the condition, defence, and perpetual security of the Kingdom of Scotland'. The business was to settle the succession to the throne. It was enacted

127

that, failing lawful male heirs of King Robert, Sir Edward and his lawful male heirs should succeed; failing these, Marjory; and failing Marjory, the nearest lineal heir of the body of Robert. In case the heir were a minor, Randolph was to be guardian of both heir and realm. Failing all these heirs, Randolph was to be guardian until parliament should determine the succession. Presently Marjory married Sir Walter the Steward. She died in her first confinement on 2 March 1316, leaving a son, who became Robert II of Scotland.

The settlement no doubt was influenced by the imminence of a large expansion of policy – the ill-starred Irish expedition. On 25 May 1315, Sir Edward Bruce landed at Carrickfergus with 6000 men. On his staff were some of the foremost Scots knights – Randolph, Sir Philip de Mowbray, Sir John de Soulis, Sir John the Steward and many others. The true motives of the enterprise are by no means clear. There was no immediate object in dividing the English forces, and in any case there was involved a like division of the Scots forces. The suggestion of the discontentment of the Scots with their territorial boundaries, growing out of repeated successes in the field and a superfluity of money, seems to be a mere speculation of the Lanercost chronicler. There is more probability in Barbour's assertion that Sir Edward Bruce, 'who stouter was than a leopard, thought Scotland too small for his brother and himself'. It may be that this particular outlet for his restless and ambitious spirit was opened up by an offer of the crown of Ireland by independent Ulster kinglets either in the first place to King Robert or directly to Sir Edward himself. It is not improbable, however, that the movement may have been a serious attempt at a great flank attack on England. Walsingham mentions a rumour that, if things went well in Ireland, Sir Edward would at once pass over to Wales. 'For these two races,' he says, 'are easily stirred to rebellion, and, taking ill with the yoke of servitude, they execrate the domination of the English.'

The Irish expedition dispatched from Ayr, King Robert and his lieutenants again turned to the Border. At the end of May, a meeting of the clergy and magnates of the north had been convened at Doncaster by the Archbishop of York at the instance of the Earl of Lancaster and other barons who appear to have been in a conciliatory mood; and on 30 June Edward issued his summons for the muster at Newcastle by the middle of August. But already, on 29 June, Douglas had entered the episcopate of Durham. Pushing on to Hartlepool, he occupied but did not burn the town, the people taking refuge on ships, and he returned laden with plunder. Sir Ralph FitzWilliam had given Edward a week's warning, but nothing had been done in consequence. It does seem odd, therefore, to stumble on an account of payment to nineteen smiths of Newcastle for 'pikois', 'howes' and other instruments sent to Perth in August.

On 22 July Bruce himself besieged Carlisle which was held by the redoubtable Harcla. His army was amply supplied by forays into Allerdale, Coupland and Westmorland. Every day an assault was delivered upon one of the three gates of the city and sometimes upon all at once, but the besieged replied manfully with showers of stones and arrows. On the fifth day of the siege, the Scots brought into action a machine that hurled stones continuously at the Caldew gate and the wall, but without effect, and the defenders answered with seven or eight similar machines as well as with springalds for hurling darts and slings for hurling stones, 'which greatly frightened and harassed the men without'. The Scots next erected a wooden tower overtopping the wall, whereupon the besieged raised over the nearest tower on the wall a similar wooden tower overtopping the Scots one. But the Scots tower proved useless for its wheels stuck in the mud of the moat and it could not be got up to the wall. Nor could the Scots use their long scaling ladders or a sow they had prepared to undermine the wall. They could not fill up the moat with fascicles, and when they tried to run bridges of logs on wheels across the moat, the weight of the mass, as with the tower, sank the whole construction in the mud.

On the ninth day, Bruce abandoned his engines and delivered a general assault, but still the besieged made manful defence. Next day the attack was renewed with special vigour on the eastern side while Douglas with a determined band attempted to scale the wall on the west at its highest and most difficult point where an assault would not be expected. His men mounted the wall under the protection of a body of archers, but the English tumbled down ladders and men, killing and wounding many and baffling the attack. On 1 August), the siege was raised. The Lanercost chronicler affirms that only two Englishmen were killed and a few wounded during the eleven days' siege.

Whether Bruce was hopeless and disgusted or had been informed of the approach of a relieving force under Valence or had heard the false report of the defeat and death of Sir Edward in Ireland, at any rate he hurried back to Scotland. Harcla promptly set out in pursuit, harassing flank and rear and making two important captures – Sir John de Moray and Sir Robert Baird. Moray had been conspicuous at Bannockburn and had been enriched by the ransom of twenty-three English knights, besides squires and others who had fallen to his share. Baird is described as 'a man of the worst will towards Englishmen'. Harcla delivered the prisoners to

Edward, receiving (8 November) a guerdon of 1000 marks, but the money was to be raised from wardships, and the payment of it was spread over eight years.

There is very little news of the Scots navy in those days, but it seems to have been reasonably active. On 12 September, one bold mariner, Thomas Dunn, 'with a great navy of Scots', followed an English ship into Holyhead harbour and, in the absence of the master on shore, carried it off to Scotland. About the same time John of Argyll was in Dublin, impatiently expecting reinforcements from the Cinque Ports. Edward retained part of the squadron to assist the French king against the Flemings.

On 15 January 1316, Bruce and Douglas made a sudden attack on Berwick by land and sea simultaneously during the night. They hoped to effect an entrance from the sea, at a point between the Brighouse and the castle where there was no wall. The attempt failed. It was bright moonlight and the assailants were promptly observed and repulsed. Sir John de Landells was slain and Douglas himself escaped with difficulty in a small boat.

The garrison of Berwick had only too much reason to complain. Writing on 3 October, Edward's Chamberlain of Scotland had informed him that the provisions expected from Boston at the end of July had never been sent and 'the town is in great straits, and many are dying from hunger'. Indeed, 'if the Mayor and himself had not promised the garrison food and clothing for the winter, they would have gone.' Two days later, Sir Maurice de Berkeley, the warden, wrote that the town and the inhabitants never were in such distress, 'and will be this winter, if God and the King don't think more of them', and quickly. Unless money and provisions arrive by the end of the month, they will give up their

131

posts and leave the town to a man. On 30 October, indeed, a vessel had brought in malt, barley and beans, but the master had had to throw overboard a great part of his cargo to escape the enemy. On 26 November, Edward sent £300 by way of pay to the garrison, but he could not aid them effectually, and apparently Valence, who was warden north of Trent, had fallen into a lethargy. The repulse of Bruce was therefore signally creditable to the defence.

A series of four official dispatches during the latter half of February and the first week in March show the deplorable state of the town because of famine. On 14 February, part of the garrison, in the teeth of the warden's orders, had gone out on a foray, declaring it was better to die fighting than to starve. They had captured many prisoners and cattle, but Douglas, on the information of Sir Adam de Gordon, who had recently changed sides, caught them at Scaithmoor, slew their leader and furiously broke up their schiltron, killing or capturing twenty men-at-arms and sixty foot. Considering that the men were struggling to keep the means of rescuing them from starvation, Barbour may well be right in declaring it to be the hardest fight that Douglas ever fought. The foray brought no relief to the garrison except by reducing the number of mouths to be fed. The men were 'dying of hunger in rows on the walls'. 'Whenever a horse dies,' wrote Sir Maurice de Berkeley, 'the men-at-arms carry off the flesh and boil and eat it, not letting the foot soldiers touch it till they have had what they will. Pity to see Christians leading such a life.'

Meantime Sir Henry de Beaumont, warden of the March, had gone to Lincoln to represent to the king and council his conferences with some of the Scots leaders for a truce. On 22 February, Edward appointed commissioners to treat with

132

Bruce, Sir Maurice de Berkeley being one, and on 28 April 1316 he authorized safe-conducts for the Scots envoys. But the business did not get forward, and the Mayor of Berwick, on 10 May, sent urgent news to the king. Berwick has provisions for a month only; the enemy's cruisers have cut off supplies and have just captured two vessels with victuals; the warden will serve an extended term only until Whitsunday; Bruce will be at Melrose in a fortnight with all his force. And all the time Edward was hampered in his measures against Scotland by the war in Ireland and a rising in Wales.

At midsummer 1316, the Scots again crossed the Border with fire and sword and penetrated to Richmond where they were heavily paid to abstain from further burning in the town and neighbourhood. Then they headed west as far as Furness, burning and ravaging without opposition. They carried home immense booty, many prisoners, men and women, and were particularly delighted with the quantity of iron they found at Furness, there being very little iron in Scotland. The leader of this expedition is not named.

For many years there had been great scarcity in both countries, a natural consequence of predatory warfare.

'This year,' says the Lanercost chronicler, 'there was both in England and in Scotland a mortality of men from famine and pestilence unheard of in our times; and in the northern parts of England a quarter of corn sold at 40s.' Walsingham says the distress was worst in the north, where, he heard, 'the people ate dogs and horses and other unclean animals.'

In Ireland it was still worse. In these wretched years of intestine broils, it is said, 'men were wont to devour one another'. Sir Edward Bruce had now been fighting there for a full year. With his Irish allies, he had raided the English adherents in Ulster, occupied Carrickfergus after a great fight

133

but failed to take the castle. captured and burnt Dundalk (29 June 1315), defeated the joint forces of the Earl of Ulster and the King of Connaught at Connor (10 September), besieged Carrickfergus in vain (until 6 December), marched down into Kildare, defeating first Sir Roger de Mortimer at Kenlis and afterwards (26 January) Sir Edmund le Butler, the justiciar, at Arscott, and returned to the siege of Carrickfergus, which was starved into surrender some time in the summer. On 2 May 1316, Sir Edward was crowned King of Ireland.

In autumn of 1315, and again in the following March, Randolph had returned to Scotland for reinforcements. On the latter occasion he brought Sir Edward's urgent request that King Robert would come in person, for then the conquest would be assured. In autumn 1316, accordingly, Bruce appointed Douglas and the Steward Guardians in his absence and sailed from Loch Ryan to Carrickfergus. His operations during the winter in Ulster do not appear to have advanced the cause materially, and in spring he set out on an adventurous expedition throughout Ireland.

Barbour's account, although considerably detailed, can be treated only with the greatest reserve. King Edward led the van, King Robert brought up the rear. The enemy lay in wait at Moyra Pass, 'the Gap of the North', the immemorial route of invaders north and south some three miles north of Dundalk. Edward, says Barbour, rode past the ambush. When the rear came up, two archers appeared in view, immediately suggesting the nearness of an enemy, and Bruce held back his men. Sir Colin Campbell, son of Sir Nigel and nephew of Bruce, pressed forward and killed one of them, but the other shot his horse whereupon Bruce, in great wrath, felled Sir Colin with his truncheon for disobedience,

134

which 'might be cause of discomfiting'. Emerging at length from the gorge, they found Richard de Clare with 40,000 men drawn up on the plain whom they presently defeated: in all the Irish war 'so hard a fighting was not seen'. When Edward heard of it, 'might no man see a wrother man'.

Advancing on Dublin, the Scots took Castle Knock on 23 February, two days later they were at Leixlip, in four days more they had reached Naas, and on 12 March they were at Callan in Kilkenny. The southernmost place they visited was Limerick, where they stayed two or three days. As they were starting northwards again, King Robert heard a woman's wail and on inquiry learned that it was a poor laundress who had been seized with the pains of labour and was lamenting to be left behind; upon which he countermanded the march until she would be able to accompany the army. Such is Barbour's story; let us call it, after Scott, a 'beautiful incident'. The expedition then somehow passed back to Dublin and on to Carrickfergus. It is an amazing narrative. Possibly the Bruces anticipated that they would gain over the tribes of the south and west; possibly they expected to tap ampler and more convenient sources of supplies; possibly they were trying the effect of a grand demonstration. At any rate they did not win any permanent support. 'In this march,' says Fordun, 'many died of hunger, and the rest lived on horse flesh,' and the demonstration was utterly futile. Towards the end of the march, the English hung upon the Scots but 'hovered still about them and did nothing'. Yet it seems unreasonable to blame the English commanders, for it cannot be doubted that they would have exterminated the Scots if they could. A change of Lord Lieutenant was impending, and Sir Roger de Mortimer of Wigmore, appointed to succeed Sir Edmund le Butler (23 November), was delayed by lack of outfit and did not arrive in Ireland until 7 April, when the expedition was practically over.

King Robert returned to Scotland in May 1317 after an absence of about half a year, bringing with him 'many wounded men'. Meantime his lieutenants had ruled Scotland with a strong hand. During 1316, Edward's efforts to conduct an army against the Scots had been again and again thwarted, and towards the end of November negotiations were in progress for a truce. At the same time the redoubtable Harcla had been defeated and captured by Sir John de Soulis (Barbour says) in Eskdale and was begging Edward for Sir John de Moray and Sir Robert Baird, his former prisoners, 'in aid of his ransom, as he does not see how he can free himself otherwise.' Truce or no truce, the Earl of Arundel, who was in command on the March, conceived the notion of sending a force to hew down Jedburgh Forest. Douglas, who was building himself a house at Lintalee on the Jed, took fifty men-at-arms and a body of archers and planted an ambush at a wooded pass. When the English – certainly nothing like 10,000, as Barbour estimates them – had entered the pass, the archers assailed them in the flank and Douglas struck upon the rear, killing their leader, Sir Thomas de Richmond, and routing them disastrously. A detachment that had taken possession of Douglas's quarters at Lintalee he surprised at dinner and slew almost to a man. Jedburgh Forest was left unfelled.

About the same time, it came to the ears of Douglas that Sir Robert de Neville, 'the Peacock of the North', irritated by the recurrent praise of his deeds, had boasted at Berwick that he would fight him on the first chance. Douglas instantly took the road to Berwick, marching in the night, and in the early morning he displayed his broad banner and lit up the landscape by firing several villages. Neville came at the challenge and posted himself on a hill, expecting the Scots to scatter in search of plunder. Douglas, however, advanced and met Neville man to man. It was an unequal contest. Neville fell under the sword of Douglas, his troops fled, and his three brothers, Alexander, John and Ralph, were among the prisoners captured and were held to ransom for 2000 marks each.

The English, beaten at all points on the Border, made an attempt by sea, landing a force of 500 men near Inverkeithing to raid Fife. The Earl and the Sheriff of Fife, although told of their coming, had not the pluck or the numbers to prevent their landing and retired. Bishop Sinclair of Dunkeld, however, rode up at the head of sixty horsemen, his episcopal cloak covering a suit of full armour. He scouted the earl's excuse of superior numbers and told him to his face that he deserved to have his gilt spurs hewn off his heels. 'Follow me,' he cried, 'and, in the name of the Lord, and with the aid of St Columba, whose land they are ravaging, we will take revenge.' Thereupon, casting off his cloak and wielding a formidable spear, he spurred right on the enemy, routed them and drove them to their ships with great slaughter. So precipitate was their flight that one barge was overladen and sank with all on board. Ever after Sinclair was called by King Robert 'my own Bishop', and popularly he was 'the Fechtin' Bishop'.

Bruce now had complete control of every part of his kingdom except Berwick, and the northern counties of England lay open to him at his will. It was more than time for a final peace.

CHAPTER XI

*C*ONCILIATION AND CONFLICT

On 1 January 1317, the pope declared a truce of two years between Edward and Bruce 'acting as King of Scotland' (*gerentem se pro rege Scotiae*) and denounced excommunication against all breakers thereof. By a bull dated 17 March he exhorted Edward to peace with Bruce 'now governing the realm of Scotland' (*impraesentiarum regnum Scotiae gubernantem*), representing not only the waste of good lives and property but also the hindrance to the recovery of the Holy Land and announcing the dispatch of his nuncios, Guacelin d'Euse and Lucca di Fieschi, to effect a solemn concord. Presently he drew up two more bulls dated 28 March – one to certain English prelates excommunicating all enemies of Edward invading England and Ireland, the other, to certain Irish prelates excommunicating Robert and Edward Bruce – but these the cardinals would hold in reserve until the issue of their mission should declare itself. In these bulls, King Robert is 'late Earl of Carrick' (*dudum Comes de Carrik*); Edward, by profession of eagerness to go on a crusade, and otherwise, is the pope's 'most dear son in Christ'. In view of the crusade, it was essential that Edward should also enjoy peace at home, and on 20 April the pope wrote to the chief magnates urging them to support their king with counsel and with help.

Towards the end of June 1317, the two cardinals arrived in England and were conducted with great ceremony to London. Edward had gone to Woodstock, where, on 1 July, he summoned his parliament to meet at Nottingham on the 18th to consider, before the cardinals should come to his presence, the questions he would have to discuss with them. On 27 July he authorized safe-conducts for the cardinals' party and assigned specially to the two prelates two officers of his personal staff. The cardinals started for the north, 'as the manner of the Romans is', with great pomp and circumstance. On the way, they were to consecrate the new Bishop of Durham, Louis de Beaumont, who was in their party. They were also accompanied by Sir Henry de Beaumont, the brother of the bishop elect, and other magnates. In the pride of ecclesiastical security, they treated with contempt all warnings of danger. They had an unexpected welcome to the episcopate. On 1 September, as they were passing Rushyford within nine miles of Durham – or perhaps at Aycliffe, three miles south of Rushyford – they were suddenly assailed by Sir Gilbert de Middleton and his robber band and robbed of all their valuables. Sir Gilbert permitted the prelates and their personal attendants to go on to Durham, perhaps on foot, unharmed; the bishop elect, Sir Henry and the rest he consigned to Mitford Castle – the eyrie from which he swooped upon the country around, harrying as far as the Priory of Tynemouth. Arrived at Durham, the cardinals, having duly adored St Cuthbert and venerated the venerable Bede, let loose upon their sacrilegious assailants all the powers of excommunication. The curse, says the Malmesbury chronicler, was efficacious, for, before the year was out, Middleton was captured and taken to London where he was drawn, hanged, beheaded and quartered.

The cardinals' advance messengers, and their special envoys (*praecursores*) – the Bishop of Corbau and the Archdeacon of Perpignan – had reached the Border in safety. There the messengers had been stopped. The envoys, however, were met about the beginning of September by Douglas and Sir Alexander de Seton and allowed to go on but only after handing over their letters for King Robert. They were conducted to Roxburgh Castle. There the king received them graciously, listened with reverent attention to the pope's open letters in favour of peace and replied that he would welcome a good and lasting peace whether arranged by the mediation of the cardinals or otherwise. He also listened respectfully to the cardinals' open letters. But as for the *close* letters, he positively refused to break the seal of one of them. They were addressed to Robert de Brus, 'governing the realm of Scotland'.

'There are several others of the name of Robert de Brus,' he said, 'who take part with the other barons in the government of the realm of Scotland. These letters may be for one of them; they are not addressed to me, for they do not bear the title of King.' No, he would not risk opening other men's letters. Still, he would assemble his Council and consult with them whether he should nevertheless receive the cardinals to audience, but as his barons were engaged in various distant places, it would be impossible for him to give his decision until Michaelmas (29 September).

The envoys had their apology ready. They explained that it was the custom of Holy Mother Church while a question was pending not to say or write anything calculated to prejudice either party.

'If my Father and my Mother,' replied Bruce, holding up the pope's letters, 'wished to avoid creating prejudice against

140

the other party by calling me King, it seems to me that they ought not, while the question is still pending, create prejudice against me by withholding the title from me; especially when I am in possession of the realm, and everybody in it calls me King, and foreign kings and princes address me as King. Really, it appears to me that my Father and Mother are partial as between their sons. If you had presented a letter with such an address to another king, it may be that you would have received another sort of answer.'

This caustic reply, the envoys reported, he delivered with a benign mien, 'always showing due reverence for his Father and Mother.'

The envoys passed to the next point. They requested him to cease meantime from further hostilities. 'That,' he replied, 'I can in no wise do without the consent of my barons; besides, the English are making reprisals upon my people and their property.'

In the confidence of authority, the envoys had taken with them one of the cardinals' advance messengers who had been sent on with a letter announcing the pope's coronation but had been stopped at the frontier. They now asked King Robert to grant him a safe-conduct, but he denied their request 'with a certain change of countenance', not uttering a word.

Turning to Bruce's staff they inquired anxiously, Why was this? Why, simply because King Robert was not suitably addressed. But for this blunder, he would have willingly and promptly responded on every point.

So wrote the cardinals to the pope from Durham on 7 September. They added that they expected nothing better than a refusal of an audience at Michaelmas, for even if Robert were himself disposed to receive them, it was evident that his barons would offer opposition. The friends of

141

Bruce had made no secret of their opinion that the reservation of the royal title was a deliberate slight at the instance of English intriguers – an opinion based on information from the papal court. The contrary assurances of the envoys had been worse than useless, and they despaired of further communication until the resentment of the Scots was mollified by concession of the royal title. Some time after Michaelmas, Bruce confirmed by letter the fears of the cardinals. He must have his royal title recognized. At the same time he repeated his desire for peace and his readiness to send representatives to negotiate, but when the bearer brought back the cardinals' reply, he was stopped at the frontier and had to take the letters back – no doubt still improperly addressed.

Three days later (10 September), Edward wrote to the pope from York where he had hastened on hearing of the assault on the cardinals, assuring him that he would promptly 'avenge God and the Church' and see that the prelates had their temporal losses made good.

To do the pope justice, he had been anxious to keep clear of the difficulties obviously involved in the reservation of Bruce's royal title. In his letter of 18 March, he had apologetically prayed Bruce not to take it ill that he was not styled King of Scotland. On 21 October, he sends the cardinals letters – one for Bruce explaining the former omission of the royal title and apparently conceding it now, another for Edward, begging him not to be offended at his styling Bruce King, and a third for themselves, blaming them for not telling him whether or not they had Edward's consent that he (the pope) should address Bruce as King. They are to request Edward to give way on the point and they are to present or to keep back the letters as they may see expedient.

Meantime the cardinals made another attempt. They proclaimed the truce in London and had it proclaimed by other ecclesiastics 'in other principal places of England and Scotland'. But they must bring it directly to the knowledge of Bruce. Accordingly they dispatched Adam de Newton, the Guardian of the monastery of the Friars Minors in Berwick, to King Robert and the leading prelates of Scotland to make the proclamation. Adam prudently left his papers in safe-keeping at Berwick until he had provided himself with a safe-conduct. On 14 December, he set out for Old Cambus, twelve miles off, and found Bruce in a neighbouring wood hard at work, 'day and night, without rest', preparing engines for the siege of Berwick. He at once obtained his safe-conduct and fetched his bulls and other letters from Berwick to Old Cambus; but Sir Alexander de Seton refused to allow him to wait upon the king and required him to hand over the letters. Seton took the letters to Bruce, or professed to do so, but presently brought them back, delivered them to Adam and ordered him to be gone. Bruce would have nothing to do with bulls and processes that withheld from him the title of King and he was in any case determined, he said, to have the town of Berwick. Adam, however, was not to be baffled. He proclaimed the truce publicly before Seton 'and a great assembly of people'. The Scots, however, would not take it seriously. Not the most solemn oaths could procure for Adam a safe-conduct either back to Berwick or on to the Scots prelates, and he was summarily ordered to get out of the country with all speed. So he took his way to Berwick. But he was waylaid and stripped to the skin and his bulls and processes were torn in pieces. Still Adam was undaunted. 'I tell you, before God,' he wrote to the cardinals on 20 December, 'that I am still ready as ever, without intermission, to labour for the advancement of your affairs.'

143

From midsummer 1317, Edward's officers had been kept busy on the March. About the beginning of July, Sir John de Athy had taken the Scots sea captain, Thomas Dunn, and killed all his men except himself and his cousin, from whom Sir John had learned that Randolph was preparing to attack the Isle of Man and even had designs on Anglesey where English traitors were in league with him. Before January there had been large submissions to Bruce in the northern counties, partly from compulsion of arms, partly from starvation, and the chronic feuds between the town and the castle of Berwick were dangerously aggravated by the high-handedness of the constable, Sir Roger de Horsley, who hated all Scots impartially and intensely.

At last a burgess of Berwick, Peter (or Simon) de Spalding, exasperated by Horsley's supercilious harshness, bribed with ready money and promise of lands, the Lanercost chronicler says, corrupted by Douglas, says John of Tynmouth, entered into communication with the Marshal (or the Earl of March) for the betrayal of the town. By direction of the king, the Marshal (or March) was ambushed at night in Duns Park where he was joined by Randolph and Douglas. Advancing on foot, the Scots planted their ladders unseen and scaled the wall at the point where Simon was in charge. The temptation to plunder upset the order of attack, two-thirds of the party scattering themselves over the town, breaking houses and slaying men. The opposition of the townspeople was easily overcome, but when the garrison sallied forth, Randolph and Douglas were dangerously weak. Sir William de Keith, however, exerted himself conspicuously, as became a brand-new knight, in collecting the Scots, and after very hard fighting the garrison was driven in. Bruce presently came up with large reinforcements, but

144

the castle held out tenaciously and surrendered only to famine. The town was taken on 28 March (Fordun) or 2 April (Lanercost), the castle held out gallantly until past the middle of July and even then Horsley marched out his famished garrison with the honours of war. Bruce installed as warden Sir Walter the Steward. Peter of Spalding, says John of Tynmouth, proved troublesome in insisting upon his promised reward, and on an accusation of plotting against the life of King Robert, was put to death. The allegation recalls the case of Sir Peter de Lubaud.

Edward was extremely incensed at the mayor and burgesses of Berwick who had undertaken, for 6000 marks, to defend the town for a year from 15 June 1317. He ascribed the loss of it to their carelessness, and in the middle of April he ordered that their goods and chattels, wheresoever found, should be confiscated and that such of them as had escaped into England should be imprisoned. On 10 June 1318, he summoned his army to meet him at York on 26 July to proceed against the Scots.

Meantime the Scots were proceeding with vigour against him, for soon after the capture of Berwick town, Bruce detached a strong force to ravage the northern counties. They laid waste Northumberland to the gates of Newcastle, starved the castles of Harbottle and Wark into surrender and took Mitford Castle by stratagem. They sold immunity to the episcopate of Durham, except Hartlepool which Bruce threatened to burn and destroy because some of its inhabitants had captured a ship freighted with his 'armeours' and provisions. Northallerton, Ripon, Boroughbridge, Knaresborough, Otley and Skipton were guiding points in the desolating track of the invaders. Ripon and Otley suffered most severely, and Ripon paid 1000 marks for a cessation of

145

destruction. Fountains Abbey also paid ransom, Bolton Abbey was plundered, Knaresborough Parish Church bears to this day the marks of the fire that burnt out the fugitives. The expedition returned to Scotland laden with spoils and bringing numerous captives and great droves of cattle. The Archbishop of York postponed misfortune by being too late with measures of resistance. But he energetically excommunicated the depredators, all and sundry.

On hearing of Bruce's reception of the envoys, the pope had authorized the cardinals, on 29 December, to put in execution the two bulls of excommunication prepared in the previous March. The cardinals, however, would seem to have delayed. On 28 June 1318, when the pope heard of the woeful adventures of Adam de Newton and of the capture of Berwick despite his truce, he ordered them to proceed. For Bruce, he said, had 'grievously' (*dampnabiliter*) 'abused his patience and long-suffering'. In September accordingly they excommunicated and laid under interdict Bruce himself, his brother Edward and all their aiders and abettors in the invasion of England and Ireland. 'But,' says the Lanercost chronicler, 'the Scots cared not a jot for any excommunication, and declined to pay any observance to the interdict.' In October, Edward followed up his diplomatic success by pressing hard for the deposition of the Bishop of St Andrews, but the pope found technical pleas to avoid compliance.

The Irish expedition came to a disastrous close on the fatal field of Faughart, near Dundalk, on 5 (or 14) October 1318. A vastly superior English army under Sir John de Bermingham moved against the Scots, and King Edward the Bruce, wrathfully overruling the counsels of his staff, disdaining to wait for the approaching reinforcements from Scotland and despising the hesitations of his Irish allies, dashed against the tremendous odds with his usual impetuosity.

> 'Now help quha will, for sekirly
> This day, but mair baid, fecht vill I.
> Sall na man say, quhill I may dre,
> That strynth of men sall ger me fle!
> God scheld that ony suld vs blame
> That we defoull our nobill name!'

Barbour gives the numbers at 2000 against 40,000, no doubt with generous exaggeration. King Edward fell at the first onset, killed by a gigantic Anglo-Irish knight, Sir John de Maupas, who was found lying dead across his body. Sir John the Steward, Sir John de Soulis and other officers were slain. Barbour tells how Sir Philip de Mowbray, stunned in action, was led captive by two men towards Dundalk; how he recovered his senses sufficiently to realize his position, shook off his captors, drew his sword and turned back towards the battlefield and how he cleared a hundred men out of his way as he went. John Thomasson, the leader of the Carrick men, took him in charge and hurried him away towards Carrickfergus. But the brave defender of Stirling had received a mortal wound. King Edward's body was dismembered, the trunk buried at Faughart and the limbs exposed in Irish towns held by the English. The head is said to have been sent to England to Edward, but Barbour tells how King Edward the Bruce had that day exchanged armour with Gilbert the Harper, as he had done before at Connor, and how it was Gilbert's head that had been mistakenly struck off and dispatched to England. The remnants of the Scots army reached Carrickfergus with the utmost difficulty and hastily took ship for Scotland where the news was received with great lamentation. Bermingham was created Earl of Louth

147

for his victory. It is curious to observe that his wife was a sister of the queen of Scotland.

The death of Edward Bruce disturbed the settlement of the succession, which was again brought under consideration of parliament on 3 December at Scone. Robert, the son of Sir Walter the Steward and the late Princess Marjory, was recognized as heir, with a proviso saving the right of any subsequent male issue of King Robert. In case of a minority, Randolph was to be guardian; failing Randolph, Douglas.

No sooner had the sentences of excommunication been promulgated than King Robert took measures to have them revoked or mitigated. He had good friends at Rome. Letters from these had fallen accidentally into the hands of Edward, who, on 12 January 1319, sent them to the pope by the hand of Sir John de Neville and asked His Holiness to deal suitably with the writers. A few days before, he had urged the two cardinals to press the pope to reject the applications that he heard were being made on behalf of Bruce and his friends and stated that he would presently send envoys to the pope himself. Neville was graciously received, and the pope ordered the Scots and their abettors at his court to prison. On 24 April the pope granted Edward's request for a bull permitting him to negotiate for peace with the Scots notwithstanding their excommunication. But the pressure was not all on one side; the nuncios in England boldly exercised their powers and had often to be restrained even by royal threat, while every ecclesiastical office was steadily claimed for the papal nominee. Bruce appears to have deemed it prudent to raise little formal objection to the papal appointment of ecclesiastics up and down Scotland, although some of them evidently had only a seat of thorns.

From March to May there was an interesting correspond-

148

ence between Edward and some minor states and munici-
palities on the other side of the North Sea whose people,
Edward understood, had harboured, or even assisted, his
Scots enemies. They all denied the allegation. The statesmanlike answer of the Count of Flanders, however, is particularly notable. 'Our land of Flanders,' he wrote, 'is common
to all men, of whatever country, and freely open to all
comers; and we cannot deny admission to merchants doing
their business as they have hitherto been accustomed, for
thereby we should bring our land to desolation and ruin.'

But Berwick must be recaptured. On the loss of Berwick
town, Edward had angrily summoned his forces to muster at
York on 26 July 1318. So few appeared, however, that he
was forced to postpone the expedition. On 4 June 1319, he
ordered the Welsh levies to be at Newcastle by 24 July at the
latest, and two days later he wrote to the pope that he hoped
now 'to put a bit in the jaws of the Scots'. But another post-
ponement was forced on him. On 20 July, however, he issued a peremptory order for a muster at Michaelmas. His
May parliament at York had granted him certain taxes, his
treasury being 'exhausted more than is believed', and his
good friend the pope had added a material contribution.
But the levy could not be collected until Michaelmas and
meantime the king appealed for an advance. There must
have been a favourable response, for early in September he
camped before Berwick with some 10,000 or 12,000 men,
his fleet occupying the harbour. Having entrenched his
lines, he delivered a general assault on 7 September. The besiegers hastily filled the dykes and placed their scaling ladders, but the garrison threw them down as fast as they were
raised. The lowness of the wall was not altogether in favour
of the assailants for the besieged on top could easily thrust

149

their spears in their faces. In the course of the afternoon the English brought a ship on the flood tide up to the wall with a boat lashed to midmast from which a bridge was to be let down for landing a storming party. They were unlucky in their efforts, and the ship, left aground by the ebb tide, was burned by the Scots, the sallying party with difficulty regaining the town. The fight went on briskly until night when the combatants agreed to postpone its renewal for five days.

Although King Robert had mustered a considerable force, probably as large as Edward's, he deemed it more prudent to dispatch it on a raid into England than to launch it directly against the English entrenchments. He had, indeed, good reason to rely on the skill and energy of the Steward. The five days' truce over, the English, on 13 September, moved forward on wheels an immense sow, not only covering a mining party but carrying scaffolds for throwing a storming party on the wall. By this time, John Crab, whom we have already met as a sea captain or pirate and whom the Count of Flanders presently assured Edward he would break on the wheel if he could only get hold of him, had proved engineer enough to devise a 'crane' which must have been of the nature of a catapult. This engine he ran along the wall on wheels to encounter the sow. The first shot passed over the monster, the second fell just short, the third crashed through the main beam and frightened the men out. 'Your sow has farrowed,' cried the Scots. Crab now lowered blazing faggots of combustible stuff on the sow and burnt it up. But presently another attempt was made from the harbour, and Crab's engine was hurried up to fight ships with topcastles full of men and with fall-bridges ready at midmast. The first shot demolished the top gear of one of the ships, bringing down the men, and the other ships kept a safe distance.

Meantime the general attack raged all along the wall. Sir Walter the Steward rode from point to point, supplying here and there men from his own bodyguard until it was reduced from a hundred to a single man–at–arms. The severest pressure was at Mary Gate. The besiegers forced the advance barricade, burned the drawbridge and set fired to the gate. Sir Walter drew reinforcements from the castle, which had not been attacked, threw open Mary Gate and sallied upon the foe, driving them back after a very hard struggle and saving the gate. Night separated the combatants. Barbour tells how the women and children of the town had carried arrows to the men on the walls and regards it as a miracle that not one of them was slain or wounded. But clearly the Steward could not sustain many days of such heavy fighting.

The Scots army under Randolph and Douglas had meanwhile followed the familiar track through Ripon and Boroughbridge, harrying and burning and slaying. They appear to have made a serious attempt to capture Edward's queen who was then staying near York, but the archbishop, learning this intention from a Scots spy who had been taken prisoner, sallied forth and brought her into the city and sent her by water to Nottingham. Trokelowe speaks of certain 'false Englishmen' who had been bribed by the Scots, and Robert of Reading specifies Sir Edmund Darel as the guide of the invaders in the attempt. Next day the archbishop, with Bishop Hotham of Ely, the Chancellor of England, and an unwieldy multitude of clergy and townspeople numbering some 10,000, advanced against the Scots between Myton and Thornton-on-Swale, about twelve miles north of York. 'These,' said the Scots, 'are not soldiers, but hunters; they will not do much good.' For the English 'came through the fields in scattered fashion, and not in united order.' The

151

Scots formed a schiltron and set fire to some hay in front, the smoke from which was blown into the faces of the English. As they met, the Scots raised a great shout, and the enemy, 'more intent on fleeing than on fighting', took to their heels. The Scots mounted in pursuit, killing (says the Lanercost chronicler) clergy and laymen, about 4000, including Nicholas Fleming, the mayor of York, while about 1000, 'as was said', were drowned in the Swale. Many were captured and held for heavy ransom. The archbishop lost not only his men, his carriages and his equipment generally, but all his plate, 'silver and bronze as well', which his servants had 'thoughtlessly' taken to the field; and yet the blame may rest elsewhere, for the York host appears to have fully anticipated that the Scots would flee at the sight of them. The primate's official cross was saved by the bearer, who dashed on horseback through the Swale and carefully hid it, escaping himself in the dusk of the evening. Then a countryman, who had observed the cross and watched the bearer's retreat, discovered it, wound wisps of hay about it and kept it in his hut until a search was made for it, whereupon he restored it to the archbishop. Such is John of Bridlington's story. The whole episode contrasts markedly with the exploit of Bishop Sinclair in Fife. It was contemptuously designated, from the number of ecclesiastics, 'the Chapter of Myton'.

The Myton disaster occurred on 20 September, and on 24 September Edward raised the siege of Berwick. Certain chroniclers speak of internal dissensions and particularly of a quarrel with Lancaster over the appointment of wardens of town and castle once Berwick was taken. The Lanercost chronicler says Edward desired to detach a body to intercept the Scots and with the rest to carry on the siege, but his magnates would not hear of it. He accordingly abandoned the siege, and marched westward to cut off the retreat of the Scots. Randolph had penetrated to Castleford Bridge, near Pontefract, and swept up Airedale and Wharfdale, and passing by Stainmoor and Gilsland, he eluded Edward's army and carried into Scotland many captives and immense plunder. It remained for Edward only to disband his troops and go home, as usual, with empty hands.

About a month later (1 November), when the crops were harvested in northern England, Randolph and Douglas returned with fire and sword. They burnt Gilsland and passed down to Brough under Stainmoor; turned back on Westmorland, which they ravaged for ten or twelve days, and went home through Cumberland. They ruthlessly burnt barns and stored crops and swept the country of men and cattle.

Edward began to think of a truce. In his letter of 4 December to the pope, he represents that urgent proposals for peace had come to him from Bruce and his friends. In any case, the step was a most sensible one. On 21 December, terms were agreed on, and next day Bruce confirmed them. This truce was to run for two years and the odd days to Christmas. Bruce agreed to raise no new fortresses within the counties of Berwick, Roxburgh and Dumfries. He delivered the castle of Harbottle to Edward's commissioners 'as private persons', with the proviso that unless a final peace were made by Michaelmas it should be either redelivered to him or demolished. On 25 August 1321, Edward commanded that it should be destroyed 'as secretly as possible'.

In autumn 1319, the pope, at the instance of Edward, had given orders for a revival of the excommunications against Bruce and his friends, but on 8 January 1320, he cited Bruce and the Bishops of St Andrews, Dunkeld, Aberdeen and Moray to appear before him by 1 May. The summons went unheeded – he had not addressed Bruce as King. Excommunications were again hurled at Bruce and his bishops, and Scotland was laid under ecclesiastical interdict. Meanwhile, however, the Scots 'barons, freeholders, and all the community of the realm' – no churchmen, be it observed – assembled at Arbroath Abbey on 6 April and addressed to his Holiness a memorable word in season. First, as to their kingdom and their king:

> 'Our nation continued to enjoy freedom and peace under the protection of the Papal See, till Edward, the late king of the English, in the guise of a friend and ally, attacked our realm, then without a head, and our people, then thinking no evil or deceit, and unaccustomed to war or aggression. The acts of injury, murder, violence, burning, imprisonment of prelates, burning of abbeys, spoliation and slaying of ecclesiastics, and other enormities besides, which he practised on our people, sparing no age or sex, creed or rank, no man could describe or fully understand without the teaching of experience. From such countless evils, by the help of Him that woundeth and maketh whole, we have been delivered by the strenuous exertions of our Sovereign Lord, King Robert, who, for the deliverance of his people and his inheritance from the hands of the enemy, like another Maccabeus or Joshua, cheerfully endured toils and perils, distress and want. Him the Divine Providence, that legal succession in accordance with our laws and customs, which we are resolved to uphold even to death, and the due consent of us all, made our Prince and King. To him, as the man that has worked out the salvation of the people, we, in maintenance of our freedom, by reason as well of his merits as of his right, hold and are resolved to adhere in all things. If he should abandon our cause, with the intention of subjecting us or our realm to the King of England or to the English, we should instantly strain every nerve to expel him as our enemy and the subverter of both his own rights and ours, and choose another for our King, such a one as should suffice for our

defence; for, so long as a hundred of us remain alive, never will we be reduced to any sort of subjection to the dominion of the English. For it is not for glory, or riches, or honours, that we contend, but for freedom alone, which no man worthy of the name loses but with his life.'

With this noble and resolute declaration, they appealed to the pope to 'admonish' Edward, who ought to be content with his own dominions, anciently held enough for seven kings, and 'to leave in peace us Scotsmen, dwelling in our poor and remote country, and desiring nothing but our own,' for which 'we are ready and willing to do anything we can consistently with our national interests.' But, further, as to the pope himself:

'If, however, your Holiness, yielding too credulous an ear to the reports of our English enemies, do not give sincere credit to what we now say, or do not cease from showing them favour to our confusion, it is on you, we believe, that in the sight of the Most High, must be charged the loss of lives, the perdition of souls, and all the other miseries that they will inflict on us and we on them.'

This memorable declaration was not without effect. On 13 August, the pope earnestly impressed Edward with the duty of keeping on good terms with Bruce. And on 18 August, he wrote that, on the prayer of Bruce by his envoys, Sir Edward de Mambuisson and Sir Adam de Gordon, he had granted suspension of the personal citation and of the publication of the sentences until 1 April the next year.

CHAPTER XII

$\mathcal{P}$EACE AT THE SWORD'S POINT

The Scots manifesto of 6 April 1320 presented a united and firm front to English pretensions and papal intrigues. Yet there were traitors in the camp. Little more than four months had elapsed when the Black Parliament, held at Scone on 20 August, was investigating a conspiracy to kill King Robert and elevate to the throne Sir William de Soulis, a brother of Sir John and a grandson of Sir Nicholas, one of the Competitors in 1292. Edward's emissaries had been tampering with the fidelity of King Robert's barons.

The plot still remains shrouded in obscurity. It was disclosed to the king, Barbour heard, by a lady. Gray, however, as well as John of Tynmouth, states that the informant was Sir Murdoch de Menteith, who had come over to Bruce in 1316–17 and remained on the Scots side until his death some sixteen years later; but, apart from his name, there seems no reason to suppose that he was in Edward's pay. Sir William was arrested at Berwick with 360 squires in his livery (says Barbour), to say nothing of 'joly' knights. He openly confessed his guilt and was interned for life in Dumbarton Castle. The Countess of Strathearn was also imprisoned for life. Sir David de Brechin, Sir John de Logie and Richard Brown, a squire, were drawn, hanged and beheaded. Sir Roger de Mowbray opportunely died, but his body was brought up and condemned to be drawn, hanged and beheaded – a ghastly sentence considerately remitted by the king. Sir Eustace de Maxwell, Sir Walter de Barclay, Sheriff of Aberdeen, Sir Patrick de Graham, and two squires, Hamelin de Troupe and Eustace de Rattray, were fully acquitted. Soulis, Brechin, Mowbray, Maxwell and Graham had attended the Arbroath parliament and put their seals to the loyal manifesto.

It is far from evident why Soulis escaped with imprisonment while Brechin and others were sent to the gallows. Robert may have judged that Soulis was a tool rather than prime mover of the plot; he may have regarded the long service of the culprit; he may have softened at the recollection of his brother Sir John's death by his own brother Edward's side. Brechin, no doubt, had considerable services to his credit. But his record shows grievous instability, and Robert probably had sound reasons for putting a period to his dubieties. His fate aroused painful regrets. Barbour narrates that Sir Ingram de Umfraville openly censured the sightseers at his friend's execution, obtained leave to give the body honourable burial and prepared to quit Scotland, telling the king he had no heart to remain after seeing so good a knight meet with such a fate. This story of Barbour's has been too hastily discredited.

The position of Bruce remained unshaken. On 17 November Edward instructed various high officers to receive to his peace, 'as secretly as they could', such Scots as felt their consciences troubled by the papal excommunication, and on 11 December the Archbishop of York was empowered to release all such renegades from the censure of the Church. Sir Ingram de Umfraville was re-established in his Northumberland estates (26 January) and Sir Alexander de Mowbray (18 February) and Sir William de Mohaut (20 May) obtained Edward's pardon. But Bruce was practically unaffected by Edward's subterranean diplomacy.

Openly, Edward maintained due observance of the truce, and by the middle of September 1320 had taken steps towards a final peace. The negotiations begun at Carlisle at Michaelmas were resumed at Newcastle on 2 February and continued for nine weeks, papal commissioners being present and French envoys fostering the cause of peace. But the deliberations were fruitless. The Earl of Richmond's production of a mass of old parchments to demonstrate Edward's overlordship of Scotland indicates how little the English king and commissioners realized the facts.

Throughout the summer and autumn of 1321, Edward was in hot water with the barons of the Welsh border. At the July parliament at Westminster, he was compelled to banish the Despensers, his favourites, and to send home the turbulent lords with pardon. These troubles prevented him from sending the promised envoys to 'enlighten the consciences' of the pope and his cardinals as to the wickedness of the Scots. On 25 August, however, he wrote the usual denunciatory generalities and yet again impressed on his Holiness the necessity of dealing severely with Bruce and his adherents. The summons of Bruce and his four bishops had meanwhile been postponed to 1 September, but even then they did not appear. Edward's envoys, at last dispatched on 8 December, were still in very good time. Having taken Leeds Castle in Kent and driven back the marauding Marchers to the Welsh border, he informed the pope that his domestic troubles were settling down, and, in view of an expedition on the expiry of the Scots truce at Christmas, he appealed for a subsidy from Rome. But already Lancaster was stretching one hand to Bruce and the other to the malcontents of the Welsh March.

The Marchers rose, but Edward proved himself the stronger and by the third week of January received the submission of the Mortimers. On 8 February he tried conciliation with Lancaster and also authorized Harcla to treat with Bruce for 'some sort of final peace'. Lancaster, however, received the Welsh insurgents and harassed Edward's advance but was compelled to fall back on his castle of Pontefract.

Lancaster's negotiations with the Scots had begun as early as December. His emissary, Richard de Topcliffe, an ecclesiastic, had obtained a safe-conduct from Douglas (11 December) to visit Jedburgh and one from Randolph (15 January) to come to him wherever he could find him. Randolph was then at Corbridge on a swift raid, while Douglas and the Steward advanced, the one towards Hartlepool and the other towards Richmond, harrying or taking ransom. Immediately on the junction of Hereford and his Marchers with Lancaster at Pontefract in the beginning of February before they went south to oppose Edward's advance, the rebel chiefs dispatched John de Denum with a letter to Bruce, Randolph and Douglas, 'or which of them he shall soonest find', asking an appointment for a final agreement. The precise terms proposed were presently found on the dead body of Hereford at Boroughbridge. Bruce, if not detained by illness or other serious cause, and Randolph and Douglas, with their power, shall join the earls in their enterprise 'in England, Wales and Ireland, and with them live and die in the maintenance of their quarrel, without claiming conquest or dominion in the said lands of England, Wales, and Ireland.' The earls, on their part, shall never aid Edward against the Scots and, their quarrel ended, shall do their best

159

to establish and maintain peace between the two countries on the footing of independence. Fortunately for Edward, John de Denum lost ten days in his peregrinations. He missed Douglas on 7 February and was unable to obtain his reply until 17 February. On 16 February, Randolph, then at Cavers, near Hawick, had issued a safe-conduct for Sir John de Mowbray and Sir Roger de Clifford to come to him in Scotland. In either case, the ten days were gone. But for this accident, the history of the English crown would probably have been turned into another channel.

The approach of the royal troops decided the insurgents to retire towards the Scots, to Lancaster's castle of Dunstanburgh. At Boroughbridge, however, they were confronted by Harcla on 16 March and disastrously defeated. Hereford was slain on the bridge, Lancaster was captured, tried and beheaded. Harcla was created Earl of Carlisle. 'Do not trouble yourself,' wrote Edward to the pope (25 March), 'to proclaim a truce between me and the Scots. Formerly some exigencies inclined me to a truce, but now, thank God, these no longer exist, and I am constrained, by God's help, to war them down for their broken faith.'

Edward at once summoned his army to muster at Newcastle by the second week in June, but early in May he postponed the assembly until 24 July. By that time, however, the Scots had completed another destructive raid. Before mid June, a force had crossed the western March, and at the beginning of July, Robert himself, with Randolph and Douglas, penetrated beyond Preston and ravaged the length and breadth of Lancashire and the archdeaconry of Richmond, burning Lancaster town and castle 'so entirely that nothing is left' and carrying off what cattle had not been driven for safety into the remoter parts of Yorkshire. They do not seem to have encountered local opposition. As they returned, they lay five days before Carlisle without drawing forth the prudent Harcla, and on 24 July they struck for home.

The English army followed them, entering Scotland by the eastern March in the first days of August. Robert withdrew both men and cattle from the Merse and the Lothians, either to the strongholds or beyond the Forth and lay with his army at Culross. Barbour tells how an English foraging party found only one lame cow at Tranent: 'It is the dearest beef I ever saw yet,' remarked Warenne, 'it must have cost £1000 and more.' Edward himself subsequently wrote that he had 'found neither man nor beast' in the Lothians. The English fleet failed to bring up provisions, and, on 23 August, Edward found himself with some 7000 men at Leith in the same predicament as his father before the battle of Falkirk. He was starved into retreat. Immediately the Scots hung upon his rear, and Douglas cut up an advance company of 300 men near Melrose. The English had sacked Holyrood; they now sacked Melrose Abbey, killing the prior, and burnt to the ground Dryburgh and other monasteries 'But,' says Fordun, 'God rewarded them therefor.'

Bruce instantly followed up his advantage. By the middle of September, the Scots were before Bamborough and Norham. Bamborough bought off the invaders, and on 26 September Sir Roger de Horsley, the constable, as well as the constables of Warkworth, Dunstanburgh and Alnwick Castles, received a severe rebuke from Edward for not showing fight against such an inferior force. Norham was defended by Sir Thomas Gray the elder against an inadequate body of 200 Scots. Edward displayed great energy of rebuke and counsel while Robert steadily advanced southwards. On 14 October, the English army barred the way on the ridge of

Blackhowe Moor between Biland and Rievaulx, but Bruce's rapid action enabled him to strike a decisive blow before the Earl of Carlisle, who was at Boroughbridge with 2000 (surely not, as some say, 20,000) horse and foot, join up with it, if indeed he really meant to do so.

Douglas at once offered to storm the English position, and Randolph, leaving his own division, led the way up the hill as a volunteer. The Scots were strongly opposed by Sir Ralph de Cobham, who was held to be the best knight of his day in England, and by Sir Thomas Ughtred, constable of Pickering, whose gallantry in the fight raised him to an even higher position than Cobham. The assailants were grievously embarrassed by stones rolled down upon them and by the fire of the archers. Robert supported them by sending 'the Irishry', the Argyll Highlanders and the men of the Isles to scramble up the crags in flank. At the top they were confronted by the main body under the Earl of Richmond, but they charged with such impetuosity as broke the English ranks and scattered them in flight; Gray even uses the conventional expression, 'like a hare before hounds'. ('In these days,' says John of Bridlington, 'the Lord took away the hearts of the English.') Richmond was captured and held to heavy ransom (14,000 marks). Lord Henri de Sully and other French knights surrendered to Douglas, by arrangement with whom, King Robert soon released them by way of diplomatic compliment to the king of France. Edward narrowly escaped from Biland Abbey and fled through the night to Bridlington, from where the prior conducted him to Burstwick. Sir Walter the Steward pursued as far as York. Robert occupied the abbeys of Biland and Rievaulx and divided the spoils of the English camp and the king's baggage. Then, making Malton his headquarters, he wasted Yorkshire at will, taking ransoms from Ripon, Beverley and other towns and despoiling religious houses. He returned with immense booty to keep Christmas in Scotland.

Three calamitous invasions in one year might well have induced reflection in a statesmanlike mind. They merely excited Edward's impotent eagerness for revenge. But the Earl of Carlisle, as doughty a warrior as the best, saw that the contest was both hopeless and ruinous, and on 3 January 1323, he was closeted with Randolph at Lochmaben.

There and then they drafted an agreement. The fundamental provisions were: (1) that each realm should have its own national king; (2) that the earl should aid King Robert in maintaining Scotland against all gainsayers; and (3) that King Robert and the earl should maintain the realm of England under the direction of a council of twelve, six to be chosen by each party. Then, if the king of England should assent to these conditions within a year, King Robert was to found an abbey in Scotland of 500 marks rent for the souls of the men slain in war and to pay an indemnity of 40,000 marks within ten years, and the king of England was to have the marriage of the heir male of the king of Scotland under advice of the council of twelve.

Harcla at once published the terms of the agreement, and they were received with intense satisfaction on the Border. He appears to have acted in concert with the chief officers in these parts and to have believed, or at least professed, that he acted within the terms of his commission. Edward, however, on 8 January, ordered that no truce be made without his knowledge and summoned Harcla to his presence, and on 19 January he sent a copy of the Lochmaben indenture to his council at York with the comment that it appeared to him 'fraught with great danger'. He had already (13 January)

163

instituted a search of the Chancery rolls for any authorization to Harcla to treat with the Scots. On 25 February Harcla was arrested in Carlisle Castle, and on 3 March he was tried, condemned and barbarously executed. The charge of treason, although formally well grounded, was essentially baseless, otherwise it is inconceivable that Harcla should have limited his measures of self-defence to the procurement of the formal oaths of the northern sheriffs to stand by him 'in all things touching the common good of England and the said peace'. His action was simply the action of a strong, businesslike and patriotic man, forgetful of finesse. His mistake lay in omitting to obtain express authority to treat and in neglecting either to veil his contempt for the king or to provide against his natural resentment, inflamed as it was sure to be by the envy of personal enemies.

The death of Harcla, the keenest and ablest warrior in England, did not remove the difficulties from Edward's path. In a fortnight he was treating for peace – 'was frightened, and begged for peace', according to the *Flores Historiarum* – although in his own maladroit fashion. On 21 March Robert wrote to Lord Henri de Sully, Edward's envoy:

'The king of England's letter, of which you sent me a copy yesterday, bears that he has granted a cessation of arms to the people of Scotland at war with him. This language is very strange to me. In former truces taken between us, I was named principal of the one part, as he was of the other part, although he did not vouchsafe to me the title of King. But on this occasion, no more mention is made of me than of the least person in my realm; so that, in case of a breach, I should be no more entitled than another to demand redress. Do not be surprised, then, that I do not agree to this truce. If, however, it were put before me in the proper way, I should willingly sanction it, as I promised you. I send you a copy

of the King's letter; for I imagine you have not seen it, or, if you
have, you have paid but scant attention to its terms.'

After some futile negotiations at Newcastle, a truce was at
last concluded at Bishopsthorpe, near York, to last until 12
June and for thirteen years thereafter. On 30 May 1323
Edward ordered it to be proclaimed throughout England,
and on 7 June Robert ratified it at Berwick. Each party was
to evacuate all lands of the other by 12 June; neither party
was to build or repair fortresses on the March except con-
structions in progress; and Edward was to interpose no ob-
stacle to any attempt of Robert and his friends to obtain absolution at Rome. During the negotiations, Edward had
been summoning his forces in England, Ireland and Gascony
in the belief that the Scots were really planning another invasion; but in the first days of June he countermanded the
muster.

King Robert was sincerely anxious to set himself and his
people right with the Church. He dispatched Randolph as
his ambassador. On his way south, Randolph, with the
Bishop of St Andrews, treated with Edward's commissioners
for a final peace, and, at any rate, on 25 November, he got
Edward to write to the pope and the cardinals in favour of a
grant of absolution to the Scots during the peace negotiations. How Randolph fared at Rome we learn from a letter
of the pope's to Edward dated 1 January 1324. First, he
begged for the usual indulgences necessary to enable him to
fulfil his vow to go on a crusade. The pope refused: there
would be little good to the Holy Land or to his own soul,
while he lay under the Church's censure. But the request
might be reconsidered if he would effect a permanent peace
with England and satisfy the Church. Secondly, Randolph

165

prayed for safe-conducts for Bruce's envoys, presently to be sent to procure reconciliation with the Church. The pope refused for the present but agreed to direct the usual application to the princes on the line of route. Thirdly, Randolph put forward Robert's readiness to join the king of France in his proposed crusade or, if the king of France did not go, then to go himself or send Randolph. The pope replied that reconciliation with the Church was an indispensable condition. Fourthly, Randolph declared that King Robert and himself desired above all things to obtain peace and reconciliation and that it really lay with his Holiness to bring their ardent desires to fruit. Let him address himself to Robert as King and Robert would readily respond to his wishes; it was the reservation of the royal title that blocked the way. The pope consented to address Robert by the royal title.

Edward was keenly annoyed. The pope, after setting forth the facts of Randolph's interview, had earnestly begged Edward not to take it ill that he had consented to address Robert as King. It could do him no harm; it could do Robert no good. He was intensely anxious for peace and if he did not give Robert the royal title, Robert would not look at his letters any more than he had done before. But Edward did not agree. He bluntly urged that the concession would prejudice his right and his honour, bring discredit on the Church and enable Bruce to make capital of his wrongdoing. He recapitulated his claims to Scotland, contended that no change should be introduced during the truce and pointed out that the concession would be popularly construed as a papal confirmation of Bruce's title. Let the title therefore be reserved as before.

Then Edward played another card: he invited Edward de Balliol, son of ex-King John, to come over to England. The safe-conduct was issued on 2 July, and it was not Edward's fault that Balliol postponed his visit. Meantime, in the midst of conflict with France over Aquitaine, Edward continued negotiations with Robert for final peace. But no agreement could be reached. The true cause appears in Edward's letter of 8 March 1325 to the pope. There had recently been a meeting of envoys at York, but the Scots would not yet budge from their old position, and 'I could not meet their wishes without manifest disherison of my royal crown.' His envoys had proposed to refer the knotty point to the decision of his Holiness, but 'this they absolutely declined'. The Scots, indeed, had apparently stiffened their demands. According to the Monk of Malmesbury, they had claimed not only the independence of Scotland but also the north of England down to the gates of York (by right of conquest) and the restoration of Bruce's manor of Writtle in Essex as well as of the famous coronation stone.

In May, Scots envoys were again on the road to Rome, and Edward wrote to the pope informing him that he was sending ambassadors to guard his own interests. Again, on 23 September, he wrote to the pope and the cardinals urging them not to recall the sentences of excommunication until the Scots surrendered Berwick to him – Berwick, captured treacherously in defiance of the papal truce. The pope consented, and on 18 October Edward expressed effusive thanks. But he reaped no advantage from the diplomatic victory: in three months he was deposed by his parliament for notorious incompetence.

On 25 January 1327, Edward, Prince of Wales, a boy of fifteen, was proclaimed king. He presently confirmed the thirteen years' truce (15 February) and appointed envoys to treat for final peace (4 March). The meeting was to take place on the March on 17 May. But on 5 April, Edward III summoned his power to be at Newcastle by 18 May, averring that he had sure information that Robert was massing his troops on the Border with the intention of invading England if his own terms of peace were not conceded. It seems much more likely that Robert's action was purely precautionary in view of the disturbed condition of the English March, but a hostile construction was favoured by the fact that many of the most turbulent fellows in Northumberland were Scots. On the other hand, Barbour is likely enough to be right in asserting that Robert was unable to obtain redress for the seizure of Scots vessels in English and Flemish waters, and it may be, as he says, that for this reason Robert openly renounced the truce. At the same time, Robert must have heard of Edward's warlike preparations by land and sea. This may be what Fordun has in view when he says that the duplicity of the English was at length laid bare. Edward's summons was issued on 5 April, and Froissart places Robert's formal defiance 'about Easter' (12 April), but this date must be nearly two months too early. One thing is certain: Robert was in no aggressive mood and would not have resumed hostilities without really serious provocation.

About the middle of June a body of Scots crossed the Border and on 4 July they were at Appleby, almost in touch with the Earl Marshal. Edward was at York, where he had been joined by Sir John of Hainault, Lord of Beaumont, with a body of heavy cavalry between whom and the English archers much bad blood had been spilled in the streets of York. His army was very large – Barbour says 50,000, Froissart says upwards of 40,000 men-at-arms, Murimuth says three times as large and strong as the Scots army – a force difficult alike to handle and to feed in a rough and wasted country, especially in face of the Scots veterans. On 13 July Edward had reached Northallerton and had learned that the Scots intended to mass their forces near Carlisle.

By this time the Scots army under Randolph and Douglas had ravaged Coquetdale and penetrated into the episcopate of Durham. When Edward reached Durham city, he was apprised of the passage of the Scots by a track of smoking ruins and devastated fields. He decided to bar their return. Advancing with his cavalry, he crossed the Tyne at Haydon Bridge (26 July), leaving his infantry on the south side. But the Scots did not come, and between drenching rains and lack of provisions his troops were worn out in body and in temper. The men, says Froissart, 'tore the meat out of each other's hands' and 'great murmurs arose in the army'. After a week of this, he determined to seek the enemy southwards and offered a reward of £100 a year in land, as well as a knighthood, to the man who brought him in sight of them 'on hard and dry ground' fit for battle. He crossed the Tyne at Haltwhistle, losing many men in the swollen river. On the fourth day, Thomas de Rokeby reported the Scots and brought Edward face to face with them on the Wear.

The Scots were strongly posted on rising ground on the south bank: Froissart numbers them 24,000, Barbour much more, probably 10,000. Douglas made a reconnaissance and reported a strong army in seven divisions. 'We will fight them,' cried Randolph, 'were they more,' but Douglas counselled patience. Presently Edward sent heralds offering to retire far enough to allow the Scots room to array themselves for battle on the north side on the morrow or, if the Scots preferred, to accept similar terms on the south side. It was an unconscious repetition of the offer of Tomyris, queen of Massagetai, to Cyrus on the Araxes river. But the Scots, evidently too weak to fight in a plain field, replied that they would do neither the one thing nor the other, that the king and his barons saw they were in his kingdom and had burnt and pillaged wherever they had passed and that if this displeased the king, he might come and amend it, 'for they would tarry there as long as they pleased.' That night the English lay on their arms. Part of the Scots also kept themselves in readiness while the rest retired to their huts, 'where they made marvellously great fires, and, about midnight, such a blasting and noise with their horns that it seemed as if all the great devils from hell had been come there.'

The next two days the Scots and English lay watching each other across the Wear. On the first day, a thousand English archers, supported by men-at-arms, attempted to draw the Scots. Douglas, planting an ambush under the Earl of Mar (who had at length joined the Scots) and his own son, Archibald of Douglas, rode forward with a cloak over his armour and gradually gave way to their onset until he had enticed them within reach of the ambush. At Douglas's signal, the ambush broke upon the pursuers and slew 300 of them. Next day, the English put 1000 horsemen in ambush in a valley behind the Scots position and delivered a front attack. Douglas was advancing to repel the assailants when he was informed of the force in the rear and instantly drew back his men. 'They flee,' cried some Englishmen, but John of Hainault explained the manoeuvre and, according to Barbour, pronounced the Scots captain fit 'to govern the Empire of Rome'.

On the following morning – probably 3 August – the Scots were gone. They had moved about two miles along the river and occupied a still stronger position in Stanhope Park. In the afternoon the English were again facing them. About midnight, Douglas, with 200 horsemen – Barbour says 500

– crossed the Wear and rode boldly into the English camp. 'No guard, by St George!' he exclaimed on being discovered, as if he were an English officer. He made right for the king's pavilion and, shouting his war cry, actually 'cut two or three of its cords'. The king narrowly escaped capture or death. Douglas got clear with only an insignificant loss and, collecting his men by a prearranged note of his horn, returned to camp. Randolph, who was waiting under arms, ready for rescue or aid, eagerly asked the news. 'Sir,' replied Douglas, 'we have drawn blood.'

The success of Douglas suggested to Randolph that a larger party might have inflicted defeat on the English. Douglas had his grave doubts. Randolph again proposed a pitched battle. Douglas objected in view of the disastrous effects in the case of defeat. No, better treat the English as the fox treated the fisherman. The fox had entered the fisherman's cottage and was eating a salmon. The fisherman discovered him and stood on the threshold with a drawn sword in his hand. The fox, seeing the fisherman's cloak on the bed, dragged it into the fire. Thereupon the fisherman rushed to save his cloak and the fox bolted out through the unguarded door. Douglas, in fact, had planned a mode of escape, and although somewhat wet ('sumdele wat'), it would serve. Randolph gave way. So the Scots made merry in the daytime, burnt great fires at night and blew their horns 'as if all the world were theirs'. Occasional skirmishes took place, and the English drew round the Scots on both sides, leaving their rear open on a morass believed to be impassable. Meantime Douglas made his preparations.

It was probably on the night of 6–7 August that Douglas led the Scots army out of Stanhope Park. He took them across the morass, about a mile wide, over a causeway of branches which the rear demolished as they passed. The men led their horses and only a few baggage animals stuck fast. By daybreak the Scots were far on the way homewards. The English had been completely outwitted. On the day before, they had captured a Scots knight who told them that orders had been issued 'for all to be armed by vespers and to follow the banner of Douglas', he did not know where. The English lords suspected a night attack and remained under arms. In the morning, two Scots trumpeters, who had been left to blow misleading blasts, were brought into camp. 'The Scots,' they said, 'are on the march home, since midnight; they left us behind to give you the information.' The English, fearing a ruse, continued to stand to their arms till their scouts confirmed the mortifying intelligence.

The Scots were soon met by a considerable body of their countrymen under the Earl of March and Sir John the Steward. They all hurried back to Scotland by the western march. The English retired to Durham and then to York, where the army was disbanded on 15 August. Edward is said to have shed bitter tears over the collapse of his expedition. Some of the chroniclers allege unsupported charges of treachery and mistakenly accuse Mortimer of accepting a heavy bribe to wink at the escape of the Scots. But the plain fact is that the English were outgeneralled at every turn.

It was neither age nor sickness, as the chroniclers allege, that prevented King Robert from leading the Weardale foray. He was away in Ireland creating a diversion. On 12 July, at Glendun in Antrim, he granted a truce for a year to Henry de Maundeville, the English seneschal of Ulster, and his people on condition of their delivering a certain quantity of wheat and barley at Lough Larne. The expedition does not seem to have been directly prosperous, the Irish, whom he had expected to rise and join him in Ulster, having apparently broken faith.

Immediately on the return of the Scots from Weardale, King Robert passed into Northumberland. He sent Randolph and Douglas to besiege Alnwick Castle, set down another division before Norham Castle and, with a third body, himself overran the neighbourhood. He even granted away the English lands to his chief followers. The attempt on Alnwick was unsuccessful, and having bought a truce, the leaders concentrated on Norham. On 1 October, while Bruce still lay before Norham, Edward appointed commissioners to treat with him for final peace. After negotiations at Newcastle and York, the treaty was signed by Robert at Edinburgh on 17 March, confirmed by the English parliament on 24 April and finally, on 4 May, signed by Edward at Northampton. Edward conceded in the fullest terms the absolute independence of Scotland as the Marches stood in the days of Alexander III and agreed to deliver up all extant documents relating to the overlordship, and in any case to annul them, and he consented to aid Robert to obtain the revocation of the papal processes. Robert agreed to pay £20,000 sterling in three years. And the peace was to be cemented by the marriage of David, the Scots heir apparent, a boy of four, with Joan, King Edward's sister, a girl of six. In England, the peace was freely stigmatized as 'shameful' and the marriage as 'base', partly on patriotic grounds, partly from dislike of Queen Isabella and Mortimer who guided the policy of the king. The news of the death of the king of France no doubt gave an impulse to the English decision, for it would be necessary for Edward to have his hands free to assert his claim to the succession. The conditions were alike 'honourable for the Scots and necessary for England'.

CHAPTER XIII

*T*HE HEART OF THE BRUCE

King Robert the Bruce died at Cardross on the Clyde on 7 June 1329, a little more than a month before the completion of his fifty-fifth year. The cause of his death is said to have been leprosy. Barbour says it was the development of a severe cold, a benumbment contracted in the hardships of his early wanderings. Apart from specific disease, the strain of his laborious reign of nearly a quarter of a century would have shaken the strongest constitution.

In the last three years he had been struck by two severe bereavements: the death of his son-in-law, Sir Walter the Steward, a knight of great promise, on 9 April 1326, and the death of the queen at Cullen on 26 October 1327. In the latter year, indeed, in spite of increasing illness, he had taken the field in Ireland and in Northumberland. But he had been unable to attend the marriage of David and Joan at Berwick in July 1328. Still he continued to move about quietly. When, however, Douglas brought him back from a visit to Galloway at the end of March 1329, it was not to be concealed that 'there was no way for him but death'. And, accordingly, he set his house in order.

On 15 October 1328, the pope had at last granted absolution to Robert from the excommunication pronounced by the cardinals and on 5 November authorized his confessor to give him plenary remission in the hour of death.

174

At a parliament held on 14 November 1328 at Scone, it had been settled that in the event of David's dying without a male heir Robert the Steward, son of Marjory, should succeed and that if King Robert died during David's minority, Randolph should be regent, and, failing Randolph, Douglas. David and Joan were crowned and David received homage and fealty.

On 11 May 1329, the king assembled his prelates and barons to hear his last wishes. He gave directions for liberal largess to religious houses, with special consideration for Melrose Abbey, where he desired his heart to be buried. He declared his long cherished intention – Froissart says his 'solemn vow' – after bringing his realm to peace, 'to go forth and war with the enemies of Christ, the adversaries of our holy Christian faith.' As he had been unable to carry out his fixed purpose, he wished his heart to be taken and borne against the foes of God. On Douglas was laid this great and noble charge. Froissart mentions a specific instruction: 'I wish that you convey my heart to the Holy Sepulchre where our Lord lay, and present it there, seeing my body cannot go thither. And wherever you come,' added the king, 'let it be known that you carry with you the heart of King Robert of Scotland, at his own instance and desire, to be presented at the Holy Sepulchre.' Douglas solemnly pledged himself to this last faithful service.

On the death of King Robert, his heart was embalmed and enclosed in a silver casket 'cunningly enamelled', which Douglas always carried about his neck. Strangely enough, even in death, the king came into conflict with Rome, for the excision of his heart was a breach of a papal bull of 1299, involving excommunication of the mutilators and excluding the body from ecclesiastical burial. On 13 August 1331, the

175

pope, at the plea of Randolph, granted absolution to all who had taken part 'in the inhuman and cruel treatment' of the king's body.

The body was embalmed and carried through the Lennox and by Dunipace and Cambuskenneth to repose with the body of the queen in Dunfermline Abbey – since Malcolm Canmore, the last resting place of the kings of Scotland. Over the king's grave was erected a marble monument that he had ordered from Paris a year before his death. It might have been supposed that never would a Scotsman lay a rude hand on the sepulchre of the greatest of Scottish kings, yet on 28 March 1560, a rabble of 'Reformers' razed the abbey to the ground and broke the royal monument in pieces. In 1818, when foundations for a new church were being cleared, in a grave in front of the spot where the high altar of the Abbey Church had stood, were found the bones of a man whose breastbone had been sawn asunder and who had been buried in fine linen shot with gold thread. The probability that these were the bones of Bruce was enhanced by the surrounding fragments of black and white marble, well polished, carved and gilt. Also found was a mouldering skull that five centuries before may have held the powerful brain that dominated the field of Bannockburn.

Douglas set about his preparations. Now that peace with England was established and Randolph held the reins of state, there was no national reason why Douglas could not be spared for a time. Nor would warriors like Bruce and his paladins have ever weighed for a moment the risks of the sacred mission. It seems a misapprehension to suggest either selfishness or ingratitude on the part of the dying king. Nor is there any substantial ground for imagining that Robert feared any lack of harmony between his two great lieutenants. Barbour's casual suggestion of petty rivalry between them cannot weigh for a moment against their constant association in scores of enterprises. Their rivalry was of noble quality. The king had made a knightly vow, and that vow he must, as far as might be, perform; it was hardly less a national than a personal obligation.

On 1 September Douglas obtained from Edward III letters of protection for seven years and a letter of commendation to Alfonso XI, king of Castile and Leon. On 1 February 1330, the day of the patron saint of his house, St Bride, he bestowed lands on the Abbey of Newbattle to secure her special intercession in his spiritual interests. Shortly thereafter he set out on his mission with 'a noble company' – one knight banneret, seven other knights, twenty-six squires and a large retinue. According to Froissart, he sailed from Montrose to Sluys, where he stayed twelve days, thinking he might be joined by other knights 'going beyond the sea to Jerusalem', and then to Valencia in Spain. According to Barbour he sailed from Berwick direct to Seville. In any case, he proceeded to the camp of Alfonso, then on his frontier warring against Osmyn, the Moorish king of Granada, and was received with honour befitting his fame and his mission. The knights with Alfonso were eagerly curious to see the famous Scot, and one notable warrior expressed his great surprise that Douglas's face was not seamed with scars like his own. 'Praised be God!' said Douglas, 'I always had hands to defend my head.'

On 25 August 1330, the Christian and Moorish armies faced each other near Theba on the Andalusian frontier. Froissart states that Douglas mistook a forward movement of the Spanish troops for the onset of battle and charged the Moors furiously, but the Spaniards had halted and left him unsupported. The story seems little consonant with Douglas's warlike intelligence. Barbour says that Alfonso assigned to Douglas the command of the van – which is very unlikely, unless he also assigned him an interpreter. He also asserts that Douglas hurled the precious casket 'a stone-cast and well more' into the ranks of the enemy, exclaiming:

> '"Now pass thou forth before
> As thou wast wont in field to be
> And I shall follow, or else dee,"'

and that he fought his way to it and recovered it, 'taking it up with great daintie'. This, too, is only a fantastic embellishment. Barbour, of course, proceeds to rout the Moors and to make Douglas press on ahead of his company, attended by only ten men. Seeing Sir William de St Clair surrounded, however, Douglas spurred to his friend's rescue but was overpowered by numbers and slain. Among those that fell with him were Sir William de St Clair and Sir Robert and Sir Walter Logan.

The bones of Douglas were brought home by Sir William de Keith, who had been kept out of the battle by a broken arm, and were buried in the church of St Bride of Douglas. The silver casket with the heart of Bruce was buried by Randolph 'with great worship' in Melrose Abbey.

Douglas has been charged with breach of trust. It is argued that he ought not to have gone to Spain but to have crossed the continent to Venice or the south of France and made direct for Jerusalem. It is hardly worth while to remark that this is just what Boece says he did, his death taking place in Spain on his way home. It is more to the purpose that the Holy Sepulchre was then in the hands of the Saracens and that Spain was the central point of opposition

178

to the infidels. But what Douglas ought or ought not to have done depends solely on the precise terms of his trust, and it may be taken as certain that he knew King Robert's mind better than either Barbour or Froissart, or even their critics, and that he decided on his course in consultation with Randolph and the other magnates, prelates as well as barons. Edward's safe–conduct and commendatory letter show by their terms that his going to Spain was no after-thought but his original intention. To attribute to Douglas lack of 'strength of purpose' is to miss the whole significance of his career.

King Robert must obviously have been a man of powerful physique and iron constitution. The early hardships and continuous toils of his reign could not have been sustained by any ordinary frame, and his recorded feats of strength, which in the case of Wallace, have been rejected as fables, have always been accepted without question. The Merton manuscript of the 'Flores Historiarum' calls him 'a very powerful man' on the occasion of his striking down Comyn. The killing of Sir Henry de Bohun in face of both armies speaks convincingly of muscle as well as of nerve. If the bones discovered in 1818 were his, they indicate that he stood about six feet in height. 'In figure,' says Major, 'he was graceful and athletic, with broad shoulders. His features were handsome, and he had the yellow hair of the northern race, and blue and sparkling eyes.'

Bruce's outstanding characteristic, in Barbour's analysis, was his 'hardiment': he 'hardy was of head and hand'. That is to say, he was a strong, bold and resolute soldier. But with hardiment he joined 'wit' – judgment, prudence, measure, and the union of the two is 'worship'. This 'worship' was un-doubtedly the fundamental cause of Bruce's great career,

179

and the most simple and conspicuous illustration of it is seen in the dramatic episode of De Bohun's death. Fordun pronounces that he 'was, beyond all living men of his day, a valiant knight.' And Barbour sums up:

> 'To whom, into gude chevelry,
> I dar peir nane, wes in his day.
> For he led hym with mesure ay.'

It was this splendid hardiment controlled and directed by cool judgment and supported by untiring industry in details that ranked King Robert not merely as the second knight in Christendom but as one of the most renowned generals of the age. His patient drudgery of preparation, his wary dispositions, his firmness of resolution, his promptitude to mark and remedy a weakness of his own and to strike hard at a weakness of the enemy, were superbly illustrated on the field of Bannockburn. King Robert's military renown does not need the false attribution of tactical discoveries that he certainly did not make. It was not Bannockburn that showed him what infantry could do against mailed cavalry, nor was it the example of the Flemings at Courtrai. Sir William Wallace had proved the power of the schiltron before Bannockburn and before Courtrai and he is not to be deprived of the honour by the imperfect historical knowledge of Sir Thomas Gray. Whether the tactic was known in these islands before the time of Wallace or if Wallace gained the knowledge of it from elsewhere still remains to be historically demonstrated. King Robert and his generals simply practised the lesson of Wallace with notable ability. Nor did they advance beyond Wallace in the still more important principles of large strategy. But, apart from this, the Bruce's capacity as a military commander stands forth pre-eminent. And although many painful incidents inevitably stain the records of his campaigns, they are attributable more to the age than to the man. It is impossible to charge to his memory any reckless or wanton cruelty. His mind, with all its sternness, always tended to clemency, and his constitutional prudence, or measure, forbade purposeless excess.

The incessant demands of war left Robert scant leisure for internal administration, notwithstanding the diligent service of his eminently capable lieutenants. Apart from necessary inference and from incidental indications, his care for civil order and good government is conspicuously manifested in the legislation of the Scone parliament, 3 December 1318, and there is abundant evidence of his fostering watchfulness over the commercial traffic with Continental countries. The Cambuskenneth parliament, 15 July 1326, has a constitutional interest as the first great council where burgesses are known to have sat with the baronage. The trading communities were worth consultation when a heavy war tax was to be levied and the country was so cruelly impoverished. There can be no doubt that Robert's management of home affairs was watchful, energetic and liberal.

In the conduct of his foreign relations, the Bruce proved himself an adept in diplomacy. His dealings with the Continental princes, mainly in regard to shipping and commerce, were conciliatory and businesslike. His political transactions with the English sovereign and with the pope were uniformly characterized by astute perception, reasonableness to the point of generosity, courteous but rigid firmness on every essential point and fidelity to engagements.

The occupations of the king's late and brief leisure may be read between the lines of the Exchequer Rolls: how he kept open house at Cardross, dispensed gifts and charities, pottered (with Randolph) at shipbuilding, sailed his great ship between Cardross and Tarbet, built Tarbet Castle, added a wing to his mansion, tended his garden, and so forth; and how he kept a pet lion at Perth where he seems to have spent parts of his last two years.

Bruce was twice married, first to Isabel, daughter of the Earl of Mar, the mother of Marjory, secondly to Elizabeth, eldest daughter of De Burgh, Earl of Ulster, who bore him two sons and two daughters, Matilda and Margaret, after 1316, David, 5 March 1324, and John, who died in infancy. The most distinguished of his other children, Sir Robert de Brus, fell at Dupplin in 1332.

Bruce has been called by Lord Hailes (after Rapin) the 're-storer of Scottish monarchy'. The monarchy was a small matter – Bruce was the restorer of Scottish independence. But the conditions of the case are apt to be misconceived. The incalculable services of Sir William Wallace through nearly ten years of incomparably heroic struggle against the great Edward in his full vigour are too often forgotten or be-littled. But for Wallace, it is more than probable that Bruce would never have been king of Scotland. He built on Wallace's foundations.

Comyn being dead, Bruce possessed the admitted right to the crown without even the semblance of competition – a powerful aid in his enterprise. He started in the acquisitive spirit of an Anglo-Norman baron and was carried through largely by his personal gallantry, his military capacity, his consummate prudence and his indomitable resolution. Al-though the mass of the people rallied to him only slowly through many years, yet he at once won over the more ar-dent patriots and, in particular, he had the instant support of the leading prelates and, at the Dundee parliament on 24

February 1309, the formal adhesion of the clergy generally. Nor is it easy to overestimate the aid of three such paladins as Edward de Brus, Randolph and Douglas. And not the least of the grounds of Bruce's success is to be sought in the feebleness and foolishness of Edward II and the stupid oppressions practised by his local officers. Still, with full acknowledgment of these supports, King Robert was and is the central figure in the final establishment of the independence of Scotland.

Perhaps the services of Sir Edward de Brus, Lord of Galloway and Earl of Carrick, have been seriously underrated, partly no doubt through his own besetting fault. When we remember how boldly he is said to have counselled action on the return from Rathlin, how vigorously he cleared the English out of his lordship of Galloway and how ably he bore the brunt of the heaviest fighting at Bannockburn, we cannot but suspect that his glory has been unduly dimmed by the splendour of his brother and by the inappreciation of his monkish critics. The main certainty about his hapless expedition to Ireland is the certainty that he fought with the most chivalrous ardour. He was not only 'hardy' but, according to Barbour, 'outrageous hardy' – a prototype of Hotspur. His habitual exaltation of mind is well expressed by Archdeacon Barbour when he describes him faced with vastly superior numbers at Kilross:

> 'The more they be,
> The more honour all out have we,
> If that we bear us manfully.'

Undoubtedly his 'hardiment' overbore his 'wit', yet one may safely doubt whether the archdeacon was the man to take his military measure. At the very least, he must have been a

183

powerful force in urging unmitigated hostility against the English and his dash in battle must have proved a potent force on many a stricken field.

In the absence of Sir Edward, Randolph ranked as first lieutenant. He was Bruce's nephew, son of Isabel de Brus and Thomas Randolph of Strathdon. From Lord of Niths-dale, he blossomed into Earl of Moray and Lord of Annandale and of Man. As soldier, diplomat and statesman, he displayed pre-eminent ability. Barbour represents him as of moderate stature, proportionably built, 'with broad vis-age, pleasing and fair', and a courteous manner. 'A man he was,' says Lord Hailes most justly, 'to be remembered while integrity, prudence, and valour are held in esteem among men.' He survived King Robert a little over three years.

The good Sir James of Douglas ranked second to Ran-dolph only because Randolph was the king's nephew. From his early teens he displayed a gallant and chivalrous spirit, a mind set on honour and withal a conspicuous gift of strate-gic device. If we may rely on Barbour, he was even more cautious than the well-balanced Randolph, yet, when occa-sion served, he could display the adventurous dash of Sir Ed-ward de Brus and he exhibited a splendid tenacity. Accord-ing to Froissart, he was 'esteemed the bravest and most en-terprising knight in the two kingdoms'. Like most great commanders, he rendered his men devoted to him by a large generosity, not merely in division of the spoils but also in recognition of valiant deeds. Barbour tells us that

> 'He had intill custom allway,
> Quhen euir he com till hard assay,
> To press hym the chiftane to sla;'

a bold principle that often decided the fight – like Bruce's

principle of striking hard at the foremost line. After he slew
Sir Robert de Neville,

> 'The dreid of the Lorde Dowglass,
> And his renoun swa scalit wass
> Throu-out the marchis of England
> That all that war tharin duelland
> Thai dred him as the deuill of hell.'

And Barbour had often heard tell that wives would frighten
their wayward children into obedience by threatening to deliver them to the Black Douglas. The Leicester chronicler
says 'the English feared him more than all other Scotsmen';
for 'every archer he could take, either his right hand he cut
off or his right eye he plucked out', and, for the sake of the
archers, he always took his vengeance on an Englishman in
the severest form he could devise. This view is not corroborated, however, and it may be a generalization from some
particular case. But, while terrible to the enemy – 'a brave
hammerer of the English', as Fordun says – Douglas is repre-
sented as charming to his friends.

> 'But he wes nocht sa fayr that we
> Suld spek gretly off his beaute:
> In wysadge[1] wes he sumdeill gray,[2]
> And ha blak har,[3] as Ic hard say;
> Bot off lymmys[4] he wes weill maid,
> With banis[5] gret & shculdrys braid.[6]

[1] visage
[2] somewhat grey (swarthy)
[3] hair
[4] limbs
[5] bones
[6] shoulders broad

185

> His body wes weyll maidand lenye,[7]
> As thai that saw hym said to me . . .
> And in spek wlispyt[8] he sum deill;
> But that sat[9] him rycht wondre weill.'

Scott's picture of the Knight of the Tomb, while based on Barbour's description, verges on caricature.

Was King Robert the Bruce a patriot? The question, startling as it may seem, especially to trustful readers of uncritical works, may no longer be avoided.

It is not necessary to repeat the outlines of his political attitude during the storm and stress of Wallace's memorable struggle. Can it be supposed, then, that a man may become patriotic after his thirty-first year? With his assumption of the kingly office, Bruce's baronial and royal interests coincided with the interests of Scotland and it may be that some feeling of the nature of patriotism may have thus developed in his breast. The manifesto of the barons and other laymen in 1320, apart from its dramatic purpose, may be taken to indicate that the external reasons for the king's profession of patriotism were not less potent than his private reasons. Let us concede to him the benefit even of grievous doubt. For, be his motives what they may, the practical outcome was the decisive establishment of the independence of the realm of Scotland, and he remains for ever the greatest of the line of Scottish kings.

[7] lean
[8] lisped
[9] became